WELFARE AND PUNISHMENT

From Thatcherism to Austerity

Ian Cummins

I0222972

BRISTOL
UNIVERSITY
PRESS

First published in Great Britain in 2022 by

Bristol University Press
University of Bristol
1-9 Old Park Hill
Bristol
BS2 8BB
UK
t: +44 (0)117 374 6645
e: bup-info@bristol.ac.uk

Details of international sales and distribution partners are available at bristoluniversitypress.co.uk

British Library Cataloguing in Publication Data
A catalogue record for this book is available from the British Library

ISBN 978-1-5292-0389-9 hardcover
ISBN 978-1-5292-0393-6 paperback
ISBN 978-1-5292-0388-2 ePub
ISBN 978-1-5292-0391-2 ePdf

Cover design by Andrew Corbett
Front cover image: 123RF 21026047

I could not have completed this project without my wife Marilyn, my sons Elliot and Nelson, and Nelson's partner Eilidh. It is dedicated to them with love.

Contents

Acknowledgements

As with all the other projects that I have undertaken, I am immensely grateful to my friends and family for the love and support that they have offered me over the years. I owe a huge debt to my late mother, who worked incredibly hard to ensure that I was able to take advantage of the educational opportunities that I was offered. She was also a lover of books; I hope that she would have enjoyed this one. My brother and sisters have been a constant source of support throughout my life. I am fortunate to have a great circle of friends and colleagues who ensure that the latest wave of academic nonsense does not overwhelm me – a special thanks to Clare Allely, Cliff and Lisa Bacon, Elaine Beaumont and Su Massey, Stuart Bowman, George Brown, Andy Davies and Selina Todd, John Devaney, David Edmondson, Marian Foley, Maria Grant, Stephen Jones, Emma Kelly, Karen Kinghorn Martin and Penny King, Jane Lucas, David McKendrick and everyone at GCU, Lisa Morriss, Kate Parkinson and Stuart Case, David Platten, Nick Platten, Muzammil Quraishi, Jane Senior, Jonathan Simon, Jo Warner, Louise Wattis, Joanne Westwood, and Toni Wood.

I am grateful to everyone at Bristol University Press for their ongoing support of my work. I would like to thank the anonymous initial reviewers of this proposal for their detailed and constructive comments and suggestions. I have tried to incorporate them into the final version. Of course, any errors or omissions are my responsibility alone.

Preface

The election of Margaret Thatcher in 1979 was one of the most significant in British history. The fact that she was Britain's first female prime minister was one of the contributory factors. However, more significant was the fact that her election marked a rupture with the social-democratic or liberal-conservative Keynesian economic and social policies that dominated the post-war period. The Thatcher governments saw these policies as enemies, the root of Britain's decline and ultimately the cause of the economic crisis of the mid-1970s, which they exploited to achieve popular and electoral success. Thatcher had been part of the Heath cabinet in the early 1970s, which had been forced to abandon a series of radical free market policies in the face of a Miners Strike in 1972. She was determined not to be placed in such a position again. Thatcher was an ideologue rather than a pragmatist. Her ideology – a mixture of free market libertarianism and traditional Conservative social values – was even given a name: 'Thatcherism'.

This volume seeks to examine the impact of Thatcherism in the fields of welfare and penal policy. It argues that those two areas have becoming increasingly intertwined. Since 1979, the UK has seen the prison population increase dramatically. There have been some periods where the numbers incarcerated have declined but the trend has generally been upward. In developing this analysis, I have used a framework based on Rose's (1994) model of a 'history of the present'. This requires an investigation 'from the point of view of a problem that concerns one today, the diverse connections and liaisons that have brought it into existence and given its saliency and its characteristics' (Rose, 1994: 53).

The prison population is now double what it was in 1979. In addition, there is a hidden incarcerated population in immigration detention centres. Alongside the expansion of imprisonment, the welfare system has become more disciplinary. This volume argues that the Thatcherite legacy in welfare and penal policy has been this punitive turn. The major changes may have been introduced by her successors but there are Thatcherite fingerprints all over them. In shifting the debate towards the right, Thatcher ensured that the Labour Party moved with her. This is most apparent in the development of New Labour. However, there is a danger of assuming that New Labour is simply a reaction to Thatcherism. This provides only a partial explanation. Blair's communitarianism was also a key driver of welfare and penal policies. Alongside these trends, this volume outlines the development of anti-welfarism. This is a discourse that is heavily influenced by Murray's (1990) notion of the underclass. These ideas have moved into the mainstream of political debate and have become the underpinning of welfare and penal policy. If we are to move towards a more equal and just society, then we need to begin by challenging the pernicious influence of the underclass discourse, with its barely concealed eugenicist overtones.

Thatcherism and its Legacy

Introduction

This chapter will examine the ideological underpinnings of what came to be known as Thatcherism, before going on to outline the main themes in welfare and penal policy in the period 1979–90. Mrs Thatcher was an unusual British politician in many ways. She was the first female leader of the Conservative Party and subsequently the first female prime minister. In the post-war period, the two major political parties had followed broadly very similar policies when in government. These included a commitment to Keynesian economics, including policies aimed at full employment and investment in public services (Kynaston, 2008).

However, the contradictions of the social-democratic consensus were fatally exposed in the aftermath of the oil crisis from 1973 onwards. Mrs Thatcher presented herself and her policies as a clear break from the post-war period and what she saw as its failings. In doing so, she developed and exploited a narrative that the nation was in crisis and that she embodied the radical action that was required to solve these problems (Sandbrook, 2011; Moore, 2013). Her supporters, particularly those in the tabloid press, contrasted the Iron Lady with the allegedly weak and ineffectual politicians who had gone before. These, particularly her predecessors Heath and Callaghan, were presented as old-fashioned, outdated and without the political courage to tackle the long-standing structural issues that had led to Britain's relative decline (Gilmour, 1992; Young, 2013). Political rhetoric and image were key elements of Thatcherism. In the areas of welfare and penal policy, much of the Thatcherite project was completed by her successors.

The influence of Thatcherism is fundamental to an understanding of welfare and penal policy in the 25 years since her defenestration from Downing Street. The influence is to be seen in both New Labour and Conservative administrations. Thatcherism was a combination of market fundamentalism and socially conservative populism. These themes are apparent in successive government policies in the areas of crime and welfare. In particular, this chapter will set the scene for the later consideration of New Labour's social policies and its 'double shuffle' (Hall, 1998). It will be argued that these moves were the result of a fear of being seen as weak on crime but also as a 'party of welfare'. The recasting of the welfare state that has occurred over the period that this work examines can only be understood in the context of the shift to the right that Thatcherism represented. It is one of the fundamental arguments of this work that welfare and penal policy cannot be divorced; rather, they have to be analysed in conjunction.

Thatcher and the welfare state

Anti-statism was at the heart of New Right thinking. One of the key elements of the 'nation in crisis' narrative was that the welfare state had become too generous, sapped independence and was open to fraud. This anti-welfarism became more pronounced and virulent in the period of austerity but it has been a consistent feature of public discourse (Garrett, 2017). This discourse is a contemporary version of one that has existed since the inception of the modern welfare state (Welshman, 2013). Thatcher's anti-welfarism is usually located in her Methodist background, with its emphasis on self-reliance (Young, 2013). Even in an era of mass unemployment in the early period of her premiership, the unemployed were portrayed in the media as 'skivers' and so on. Comparisons were consistently made with the alleged behaviour of those out of work in the 1930s. In his speech at the Tory Party conference in 1981, Norman Tebbit, then Employment Secretary, told how his father 'got on his bike' to look for work in the Great Depression. The speech came after a summer of rioting in Britain, which had taken place in areas of high structural unemployment. However, the Thatcher government was following monetarist policies that focused on tackling inflation and assumed that there was a 'natural level' of unemployment. The anti-welfarism of the Thatcher period has become further embedded within the public discourse. In this area, the long-term political impact was to shift the debate to the right.

On the Left, the initial response to the arrival of Mrs Thatcher in government was to recognise that this was a paradigm shift (Gough, 1980); indeed, Hall (1979) had coined the term 'Thatcherism' before she was even elected. The influence of Mrs Thatcher on the political discourse is captured by the fact that an ideological position was given a name. This is highly unusual in the British political lexicon, where pragmatism is usually valued above ideology, though there were also clear attempts to outline Blairism and the 'Third Way'. At the beginning of her time in Downing Street, the aims of Mrs Thatcher in the welfare field were clear. These were to: introduce the market into areas of provision such as housing and education; reduce social security benefits and encourage work incentives; and create further divisions between the 'deserving' and 'undeserving'. Alongside these aims, there was a restatement of so-called traditional values, such as attacks on progressive education and support for law and order (Gough, 1980). Consequently, police pay was increased and there was a recruitment drive. The attack on the welfare state was an ideological as well as an economic project. Gough (1979) argues that acting in the interests of capital, the New Right sought to exploit an economic crisis to restructure the welfare state. This process would include a shift in emphasis to social control via these systems, as well as the privatisation of sections of the welfare state. This pattern was repeated by the Coalition government from 2010 under 'austerity' (Cummins, 2018). Gough (1980), like Hall (1979), provided a very prescient analysis of the Thatcherite project. One aspect of both analyses that is often overlooked is that they highlighted the popular appeal of Thatcherism, which includes an anti-collectivist appeal to those who experience the state, including the welfare state, as bureaucratic and oppressive.

The attack on the welfare state by the New Right in the 1970s was based on the combination of economic and populist ideas. The welfare state was seen to generate higher levels of taxation generally but particularly on those who were least likely to use its services. The rest of the economic case against the welfare state was that it created inflationary budget deficits and disincentives to work and save (Wilding, 1992). Alongside this, populist notions about 'scroungers' and the alleged exploitation of the welfare system by 'undeserving' immigrants and teenage single mothers were used to attack the overall notion of the welfare state. Hall (1979) notes that this ideological attack was carefully constructed and crafted, and used the moment of the economic crisis to strike. It was also electorally successful (Gamble, 1994). The Thatcher government of 1979–83 followed monetarist policies. In monetarism, the focus is on tackling inflation via control of the money supply, which requires a reduction in the public sector borrowing requirement. This aim was combined with a commitment to lower levels of personal taxation, as well as higher defence spending. The result was to place further pressure on other areas of public spending (Gilmour, 1992). High unemployment also has the effect of weakening organised labour and lowering wage demands.

Thatcherism attempted to create a new form of public sector, which included the development of quasi-market relationships between different elements of the welfare state. Wilding (1992) notes that the quasi-market system meant that there was a focus on the virtues of the market, and offered scope for further privatisation in the future. If providers did not meet the terms of their contracts, then they would not be renewed. In addition, this new organisational form meant that the government could distance itself from responsibility for service provision. The NHS and Community Care Act 1990 saw the introduction of the so-called purchaser–provider split and the development of a market in social care. Here, the notion is that individuals are no longer passive recipients of care, but consumers exercising choice. The final element of this new form of public sector was the introduction of private sector management techniques. The result was an explosion in the use of management consultants and the development of an audit culture in the public sector. These trends were not reversed by the advent of New Labour in 1997.

One of the most fundamental principles of the post-Second World War welfare state was universalism (Timmins, 2001). The pooling of social risks would create a system where benefits and services would be available to all. This notion of universalism and its link to a notion of social citizenship was anathema to the New Right. The welfare changes introduced in this period represented a fundamental challenge to the principles of universalism (Riddell, 1991; Gilmour, 1992) as there was a shift to means-test benefits. Lister (1998) notes that in 1979, 17 per cent of spending was on means-tested benefits; in 1995, the figure was 36 per cent. The Social Security Act 1986 saw the creation of the Social Fund, which introduced a series of crisis payments. The system was discretionary And loans were repaid via a reduction in future benefit payments. There were three types of Social Fund payment: budgeting loans; crisis loans for emergency situations; and community care grants to help vulnerable people live independently, which were not repayable. People could be refused loans if it was felt that they were unable to make repayments. In addition, the Social Fund was administered locally, meaning that claims could be rejected because the budget had been exhausted.

The Major government introduced changes to the welfare system that can be seen as part of an avowedly Thatcherite agenda. These included changes to Housing Benefit regulations for the under 25s and, perhaps most importantly, the establishment of the Child Support Agency (CSA). Major's 'Back to Basics' campaign – an attempt to reinvigorate so-called traditional values – collapsed in a series of scandals about the private lives of members of his government.

In the area of welfare, the Thatcherite revolution was finally completed by Tory successors. There was some rolling back under New Labour, with significant investment in health and education. However, in the area of welfare, the main themes of Thatcherism and its anti-welfarism were still clearly apparent. There was a significant ideological and rhetorical shift that saw state intervention becoming the cause of, not the solution to, a range of issues. Alongside this, there was also the creation of an individualising narrative (Wilding, 1992). The result of these changes was a significant increase in poverty. Despite the Thatcherite rhetoric, the public support for collective provision remained strong (Timmins, 2001). Opinion polls consistently showed that voters supported the proposition of increased direct taxes in return for better public services. In his review of the impact of Thatcherism, Wilding (1992: 207) concluded: 'The rich have got richer, the poor have got poorer and there are vastly more poor.' Alongside this, the successful were lionised while the poor were demonised – trends that have continued ever since.

Defining Thatcherism

The term 'Thatcherism' was coined by the late Stuart Hall in early 1979 before Mrs Thatcher had won the general election. In his path-breaking article 'The great moving right show', Hall (1979) was the first commentator on the Left to see that the arrival of Mrs Thatcher marked a hugely significant shift. It was not simply business as usual or the Tories' turn to govern; rather, Thatcher's victory in the general election of May 1979 was one of the most significant moments in modern political history. British political history, up to and including the Brexit referendum, can be read as a response to the general election victory.

Mrs Thatcher had been elected Conservative Party leader in 1975 when she defeated the incumbent Edward Heath. Heath had been Prime Minister from 1970 to 1974. Heath's shadow cabinet met in January 1970 at the Selsdon Park Hotel in Selsdon. This meeting led to the generation of radical free market and libertarian policy ideas for the forthcoming election, which were ridiculed by the then Labour Prime Minister Harold Wilson as the work of 'Selsdon Man'.

Heath won the general election and Mrs Thatcher became a member of the cabinet. However, following industrial unrest, including a miners' strike in 1972, Heath abandoned the manifesto and Selsdon Man (Sandbrook, 2011; Moore, 2013). Brought about, in part, by the miners' strike, this U-turn was seen within the Tory ranks as almost an act of political betrayal. In February 1974, Labour formed a minority government but political instability led to another election in October 1974, which led to a Labour majority of three. There was a challenge to Heath's position, and although Sir Keith Joseph was seen as the likely representative of the libertarian Right, he ruled himself out following a speech in which he said: 'A high and rising proportion of children are being born to mothers least fitted to bring children into the world. ... Some are of low intelligence, most of low educational attainment. ... The balance of our human stock, is threatened' (Halcrow, 1989: 83).

Thatcherism and penal policy

Margaret Thatcher's political persona of the Iron Lady comes from her strong anti-communist stance and the victory in the Falklands War (Young, 2013). However, before she became Prime Minister, she had cultivated the idea that she was tough on law and order. Her leadership of the Conservative Party and subsequent premiership were both marked by hugely significant events in this area: one of her political mentors, Airey Neave, was murdered in a bombing by the Irish National Liberation Army (INLA) at the House of Commons in 1979; there were riots in Britain in 1981 and 1985; the 1984–5 Miners' Strike involved police clashes with striking miners; and the Irish Republican Army (IRA) bombing of the Conservative Party conference at Brighton in 1984 came close to killing Mrs Thatcher and other members of the cabinet.

During the early years of her term in office, the nation was in the grip of the hunt for the Yorkshire Ripper. It appears at one point that Mrs Thatcher considered taking a lead role in the case (Casefile: True Crime Podcast, 2017). The Police and Criminal Evidence Act 1984 (PACE) was one of the most important pieces of legislation in this field. It established a whole new framework for the conduct of police interviews, giving those detained in custody new codified rights. Overall, it is something of a surprise to see that in the general field of penal policy, there was little in the way of a Thatcherite shift. The major punitive turn actually occurred after she had left office. One factor is that the home secretaries from the early 1990s onward, such as Michael Howard, were 'true believers' in the Thatcherite approach. One could say the same of New Labour home secretaries, such as Straw, Reed and Blunkett, who were determined not to be outmanoeuvred on law and order.

The link between the developing New Right and 'tougher' penal policy did not lead to a rash of legislation in the first Thatcher administration. Her first Home Secretary, Willie Whitelaw, was very much an old-school patrician One Nation Tory. It was somewhat out of political character for Whitelaw to support the idea of a 'short, sharp, shock' for young offenders, and it was quietly shelved after the election victory of 1983 (Windlesham, 1993). Thatcher had come to power on a manifesto that was strong on law-and-order rhetoric. One aspect of this rhetoric was the casting of industrial disputes in these terms. Trade unionists and workers on strike were presented as 'wreckers' seeking to undermine the traditional fabric of British society.

The death penalty was effectively abolished in the UK in 1965. Since the vote to abolish it, there have been fairly regular calls for it to be reinstated. For example, there have been attempts to make the murder of a police or prison officer a capital offence, alongside terrorist murders. Thatcher herself was a firm supporter of capital punishment. In May 1982, a Bill to reintroduce capital punishment was overwhelmingly rejected by a margin of 162 votes. This and a later vote took place before the full revelation of the 1970s miscarriages of justice that shook confidence in the criminal justice system (CJS). These cases included the Guildford Four, cleared in 1989 of murdering five people in a 1974 IRA bombing, and the Birmingham Six, cleared in 1991 of another 1974 IRA bombing of two city-centre pubs in which killed 21 people were killed. Since that time, there has been no real political will to reintroduce capital punishment despite home secretaries such as Waddington being supporters of it. Article 2 of the Human Rights Act (HRA) and other international commitments mean that the official UK policy has been to oppose the use of the death penalty.

In contrast to the rhetoric, the prison population fell (Windleshamm 1993). In part, this was due to the Criminal Justice Acts of 1982 and 1988, which introduced restrictions on sentencing young people. This period can be viewed very largely as an extension of the post-war consensus approach to law-and-order policy, where prison was very much viewed as a last resort; instead, the focus should be on the rehabilitation of all but the most serious offenders. For example, before the changes introduced in the 1990s by Michael Howard, the probation service was officially 'a social work agency within the Criminal Justice System' (Smith, 2005: 633). Trainee probation officers qualified as social workers, and the focus of the role was on general welfare and individual work with offenders.

Overall, the Tories may have sounded tougher on crime but the approach was essentially a bipartisan one. Later home secretaries were prepared to abandon this approach. In fact, they adopted a new bipartisan approach, which was 'tough on crime'. The first Thatcher government did not enact a penal policy based on its tough rhetoric. There are a number of factors at play here. In the first instance, there is always a gap between political rhetoric and political reality. However, Thatcherites might also argue that the implementation of policy was thwarted by so-called 'wet' home secretaries ('wet' was term of abuse that Thatcherites used for old-school Tories) (Gilmour, 1992), the liberal elite and the civil service.

The lack of what can be termed a 'Thatcherite turn' in policy does not provide a complete picture of the 1979–90 period. Hay and Farrall (2014) argue that many of the changes that were introduced in economic and social policy led directly to increases in crime. Deindustrialisation and the huge increases in unemployment are one of the key factors here. There is a strong link between unemployment and crime (Farrall and Jennings, 2012). Thus, the landscape created by the Tories in the 1980s was one that the Major government of the early 1990s had to address. This trend was also strengthened by the appointment of Michael Howard as Home Secretary in 1993. Howard's career and influence is discussed in more detail in Chapter 4. However, his commitment to a 'prison works' philosophy and a willingness to implement policies based on it represented a significant shift. Equally significantly, Howard was shadowed by a then rising star of the Labour Party, Tony Blair. In this role, Blair led a tack to the right. This shift in penal policy was a key element in the creation of 'New Labour' (Newburn, 2007). When in office, New Labour did not reverse any of the significant penal policy trends that began in the Major period. Farrell and Hay (2010) conclude that the influence of Thatcher governments on law and order should be viewed in two ways. First, just as attitudes to penal policy were a key element in the creation of New Labour, the same is true for Thatcherism. In rejecting the post-war consensus, Thatcher used concerns about crime as a way of establishing a connection with sections of the electorate. The second is that the outcome of social and economic policies of the 1980s and early 1990s was to create circumstances where increased unemployment and inequality led to higher crime rates. It was these circumstances that led to demands for more punitive approaches to crime and the policies of the 1990s.

Thatcher's legacy

A statue of Margaret Thatcher was unveiled in the Palace of Westminster in 2007. She died in April 2013 and was honoured with a state funeral.

There is no doubting her influence on late 20th-century Britain. To her supporters, she was the Iron Lady who had saved Britain from the chaos of the 1970s, presided over an economic miracle and restored the country's standing in the world. To her opponents, Mrs Thatcher was heartless, cruel and immune to the suffering that her policies had inflicted. She was, and is, such a polarising figure that there were few who remained neutral. In examining the legacy of her period in office, there is an inherent danger of focusing on her as an individual and ignoring the other social and economic factors that were important.

Gamble (1994) saw the New Right that Thatcher represented as a combination of classic free market liberalism and traditional Conservative moralism and family values. Thatcher set herself firmly against what she saw as the inevitable outcome of the social reforms and permissiveness of the 1960s. Hall (1979) noted the way that Thatcher was able to place herself alongside families. This is a discourse that continues to this today, with politicians using terms such as 'hard-working families' or 'strivers'. This establishes a binary divide as, logically, those who are not hard-working are scroungers and so on. Thatcher presents the state as being made up of progressives – teachers, social workers and members of the liberal elite – who are not only opposed to traditional values, but also despise those who hold them.

Gamble (1994) notes that there is a tension between the two main elements of Thatcherite thought. Mrs Thatcher seems to have managed or felt no difficulties with these contradictions. She famously called for a return to what she termed 'Victorian values'. This was interpreted as being rooted in the influence of her Methodist childhood. However, Bellamy (1991) argues that for someone who was supposedly a traditionalist, she was also an iconoclast. She attacked many major institutions, including the Church of England, Universities and the civil service, and limited the traditional role of local government. In 1985, her education policies so upset the dons at her alma mater, Oxford, that they voted not to give her an honorary degree. In 2000, one of her successors and fellow Oxford graduate, Tony Blair, was also denied an honorary degree for an attack on the university's elitist admission policies.

It is impossible to disentangle Thatcher's welfare and penal policies from her broader economic and social policies. The rhetoric was very much influenced by Joseph's 1975 speech, where he spoke of 'cycles of deprivation'. The speech meant the end of his leadership bid but it did not prevent Thatcher appointing him as Minister for Social Security (Halcrow, 1989). One of the most significant features of the Thatcher period was the increase in inequality. This was the result of a number of factors: tax cuts for the highest earners were combined with reduced benefit levels; while mass unemployment was a feature of the Thatcher period as the economy moved towards reliance on the financial sector and the service economy (Gilmour, 1992).

The sale of council housing and the Lawson boom of the late 1980s, which saw houses prices rise significantly and rapidly, all added to increased levels of inequality (Dorey, 2015). In the period 1979–95, the incomes of the top 10 per cent of earners rose by 60 per cent. As noted earlier, at the same time, the de-indexing of benefits, which previously rose in line with average earnings, meant that the gap between those in secure employment and the unemployed or those employed in precarious work increased. This is another modern trend whose roots can be traced back to the Thatcher years. The first New Labour government from 1997 to 2001 went someway to reversing this trend of growing inequality by investing in health, education and other public services. However, one of the last legacies of Thatcherism is that governments seem remarkably sanguine about levels of inequality. Dorey (2015) notes that Thatcher's hagiographers portray 1970s' Britain as almost on a par with a Soviet-style command economy, which is clearly a huge exaggeration. It is also interesting to note that Britain was at it most equal in the mid-1970s, before the arrival of Mrs Thatcher in Downing Street (Cummins, 2018).

The rhetorical style of Thatcherism was, in many ways, as important as its substance. The corporatism of the 1960s and 1970s was replaced by conflict and confrontation, most obviously, in the Miners' Strike but in other areas too. In later years, and perhaps even more so after her defenestration from office, this verged more towards a form of political paranoia. The title of Hugo Young's magnificent analysis of the Thatcher Years – *One of Us* – reflects the conflictual nature and stance of Thatcherism. Compromise and alliance building came to be seen as signs of weakness rather than the proper conduct of government – another baleful aspect of modern politics that has its roots in this period. It would be naive to think that there has never been scheming and rivalry in politics, for example, the revelations of the Benn and Crossman diaries show that the Labour government of the 1960s was riven by splits and so on. However, there was a change in the 1979–90 period. Mrs Thatcher was supported by the press, and the tabloid press, particularly *The Sun* and *The Mail*, became a key point of connection between the Conservative Party and working-class and lower-middle-class voters. Her Press Secretary, Bernard Ingham, had a key role here. In an echo of later debates, the Labour Party was presented as having lost contact with its core constituency.

The intellectual gurus of Thatcherism argued that inequality was an inevitable feature of free market economies. Alongside this, it was argued that free markets would inevitably lead to free societies. This conveniently overlooks the fact that the first monetarist experiment took place in Chile after the military coup. The coup saw the overthrow and murder of Salvador Allende, a democratically elected socialist president. The economic 'reforms' that the military dictatorship of General Pinochet introduced were led by a group of economists nicknamed the 'Chicago Boys', who had studied under Friedman in the US (Letelier, 1976). In the Friedman School of economics, inequality was seen as an inevitable outcome of a market economy. Furthermore, Hayek's notion of liberty (Kley, 1994) meant that he did not accept the notion of the social. In this model, distribution through the market did not involve the intentional disadvantaging of others; rather, it was simply a function of the market. The market decides on the value of skills through the mechanisms of supply and demand, and does not use any principle of justice to distribute. This approach is tied with his critique of the notion of positive liberty (Berlin, 2002 [1958]). Positive liberty argues that an individual can only be free if they are able to fulfil their goals. Hayek (2018) saw this as flawed as humans have a potentially infinite range of goals or desire. As such, it is not possible to fulfil them all and there is no objective way of deciding between competing demands. The same is true at a wider level. Therefore, the result will be that state bureaucracies make arbitrary decisions and claim huge powers for themselves, and any interventions designed to produce a more equal society will involve some form of totalitarian state and will fail (Gray, 2013).

Dorey (2015) notes that alongside the philosophical acceptance of inequality, the Thatcher years were marked by a near veneration of the rich as 'wealth creators'. Successful companies were presented as the work of one individual – usually, but not always, a white man. This was a modern version of one of the foundational myths of modern capitalism – the self-made man. Thus, success was the result of individual enterprise and talent of one person, rather than a complex range of factors, including the work of the company staff. The veneration of the rich was accompanied by pathologising and stigmatising the poor. At the same time, there was a sneering attitude to those who were in favour of greater equality. Depending on the individual's own position, it was portrayed in the popular press as the result of envy and class warfare, or guilt (Dorey, 2015). It is ironic that the Methodist Thatcher presided over the development of a wider social culture that not only tolerated excess, but celebrated it.

Conclusion

Mrs Thatcher is alleged to have described New Labour as her greatest achievement. By this, she meant that the arrival of Blair appeared to signify an irrevocable move by Labour to the 'centre ground'. This is, of course, a highly debated term. Blair may have seen himself as a centrist but his opponents viewed him as a neoliberal who, despite huge election victories, continued along largely Thatcherite lines. Even her most bitter opponents would have to accept that Mrs Thatcher's period in office marked a huge shift in British politics. There is an ongoing debate about the extent to which she was personally responsible for these shifts. The changes in the British economy, particularly deindustrialisation, would have certainly occurred whoever was in political office. However, the confrontational style and rhetoric – the creation of the Iron Lady persona – had a lasting impact. In the areas of welfare and penal policy, it is possible to argue that the changes she instigated have influenced all policy since. Hall's (1979) prophecy proved correct – there has been no going back. This volume explores how the war on poverty became the war on the poor. The first shots in that long war were fired on 4 May 1979.

2

Welfare and Punishment in a 'Stark Utopia' (1979–2015)

Introduction

Welfare and penal policies are inextricably linked and interrelated social and political phenomena, which therefore need to be analysed in unison. The reduction of the social state and the expansion in the rates of imprisonment are joint strategies by governments. The punitive shifts that led to the increase in prison populations from the late 1970s onwards in England and Wales have had a much broader influence than simply in the area of criminal justice, having helped to entrench views about the nature of marginalised groups or populations. This chapter will examine the genealogy of the penal state and the various explanations for its development. Penal policy and social provision are used to provide or give the illusion of social stability. Developments in these areas are often a response to a crisis of legitimacy. This chapter will argue that the crisis in the late 1970s that led to the advent of neoliberalism led not only to new economic policies, but also to linked new social policies that stigmatise marginal groups. The supporters of these policies argued that the retrenchment of the welfare state was necessary because of a state fiscal crisis. The spectacle of punitivism also served to convince voters that social investment was counterproductive as the management of the 'underclass' could only be achieved through coercion – in the areas of welfare and penal policy.

Welfare and penal policy and the end of history

The term 'homo economicus' is used in economic theory and modelling to represent the individual rational agent. In these models, homo economicus is a forward-looking rational agent who only pursues their own self-interest and makes decisions that are of most benefit to them. There are huge philosophical disputes about how realistic the figure of homo economicus is, though there is not the space to examine those in depth here. However, for political and economic ideas in the period 1979–2015, homo economicus was a key concept. The basis of the wider philosophy of neoliberalism is that individual rational agents will not act in ways that run counter to their own self-interest. From the conception of the figure of homo economicus much else flows. In particular, it is the basis of the attack on welfare provision, and Becker's (1968) development of rational choice theory and its application to crime and punishment is rooted in the figure of homo economicus.

Rogers (2014) argues that the real significance of Mrs Thatcher's political career pertains to her style, not the substance of her policies. He suggests that there is a danger of developing something of cult around her, with the naming of her policies as 'Thatcherism' being part of this process. The focus on personal style has become even more pronounced since the expansion of 24-hour rolling news and social media. Trump and Johnson are examples of this process, whereby much of the media coverage is taken up with responses to controversial things that they have said or public appearances that they have made. In both cases, it seems that they move on very quickly to the next one, leaving the media scrambling to keep up. Mrs Thatcher was very aware of her image. Before her election successes, she cultivated an image of the average housewife who knew the importance of balancing a budget. In office, she became, certainly to her supporters, the saviour of the nation and the Iron Lady on the world stage (Sandbrook, 2011; Moore, 2013).

The election of Thatcher in 1979 and Reagan in 1980 are usually viewed as marking the end of a Keynesian social-democratic approach to government that had been followed in liberal democracies since the end of the Second World War. The broad features of policy in this period included a commitment to full employment, expanding public services and recognising that the state could play a positive role in the lives of citizens. The Thatcher and Reagan governments were opposed to all these policies and they sought ways of reducing the public sector. Tackling inflation rather than unemployment was a key aim, and the state was to have a much diminished role in society. On the international stage, both were Cold War anti-communists committed to maintaining the West's military power, including nuclear weapons, against the Soviet bloc (Young, 1999; Fischer, 2000). Both saw the welfare state as corrosive. Finally, both were strongly committed to a politics of law and order which argued that the CJS was too focused on the rehabilitation of offenders, with the rights and concerns of victims being sidelined. These tropes in welfare and penal policy have essentially been the main parameters of debate ever since.

Thatcher and Reagan were both divisive and hugely successful. The fall of the Berlin Wall in 1989 and the collapse of the Soviet Union in 1991 were regarded as marking the ultimate victory of liberal market-oriented capitalism. In 1992, Fukuyama published *The End of History and the Last Man*. In this work, Fukuyama (1992) argued that the liberal-democratic model was the final and most complete form of ideological and governmental organisation. Liberal-democratic forms of government can cover a very wide range, including the Keynesian approaches of the period 1945–79. Given the period when he was writing, it is safe to assume that Fukuyama was using the term to mean a neoliberal model, that is, a combination of representative democracy and open global markets (Hall, 2011). Fukuyama's (1992) approach is based on a materialist conception of history. It takes an evolutionary approach to the development of political economy, concluding that all the major questions in this field have been solved as the answers to them will always be found in the application of market-oriented economics. From this open economy, liberal-democratic politics inevitably flow (Fukuyama, 1992). Fukuyama's book was an unusual bestseller and a huge success. This is partly explained by the fact that it caught a particular spirit of the times. It presented the success of neoliberalism as a form of manifest destiny, which was, of course, particularly appealing to those who were in power in the West at the time.

Fukuyama's (1992) thesis obscured the fact that neoliberalism was a long-standing political and economic project (Harvey, 2005). Hayek (2014) had published one of the key neoliberal texts, *The Road to Serfdom*, in 1944. Hayek and his followers had never accepted the post-Second World War social-democratic settlement. Far from being an evolutionary inevitability, the political success of neoliberalism was the result of a 70-year project (Mirowski, 2014). Fukuyama's (1992) materialist analysis sidelines neoliberalism as a political, economic and class project. The roots of contemporary neoliberalism can be found in the responses of the Freiburg School and the London School of Economics (LSE) to the Great Depression (Stedman-Jones, 2012: 3). The Freiburg School, later known as ordoliberals after its journal *Ordo*, argued that the state had a key role to play in the maintenance of the market, rather than intervening in it. The foundation of Roosevelt's New Deal was a Keynesian approach that saw public projects as having a key role to play in tackling unemployment (Leuchtenburg, 2009 [1963]). These political approaches, the New Deal and the Freiburg

School were developed in the social, political and economic contexts of the 1930s. Mass unemployment had led to the growth of political extremism and the consequent spectre of totalitarianism. Both the New Deal and Ordoliberals recognised the need for the state to ensure political and economic stability. Ordoliberals promoted the concept of the social market economy, emphasising the need for the state to take action to ensure that the market produced the optimum outcomes.

The most influential text in the modern development of neoliberal thought is Hayek's *Road to Serfdom*, originally published in 1944. Hayek's work ran counter to most of the prevailing dominant economic and political ideas. The demands of the Second World War had seen an unprecedented role for the state in the management of the economy. While this was justified in the context of a total war, this would not be the case in peacetime. There are two central tenets in modern neoliberalism: the supremacy of the market; and a belief in liberty as the supreme social and political value. These are at the heart of Hayek's analysis. Here, liberty is defined very much as freedom from state or other interference. The market is seen as the most effective means that has been established for the distribution of resources.

The role of the state is to ensure markets can operate. This requires the establishment of a legal framework so that contracts can be enforced. Hayek argued that taxation of all sort, both personal and company, needs to be as low as possible. There are two elements to this: low taxation encourages individuals to work harder or innovate; and Hayek saw government bureaucracies as inherently inefficient and wasteful of taxpayers' money, and so higher taxation would fund these profligate public schemes. It is important to recognise that there was one area where the state should be strong: law and order. Nozick (1974) provided a philosophical justification for the so-called 'nightwatchman state'. In the period that this volume covers, the nightwatchman state has grown significantly, while, at the same time, the social state has retreated.

In 1947, Hayek organised a meeting at Mont Pelerin in Switzerland. Here, a group of economists and other intellectuals and academics met to plot the defence of liberalism against what they saw as the forces of collectivism. 'Collectivism' was a very broad term that not only included fascist and communist totalitarian states, but also the emerging post-war social democracies of Europe. The Mont Pelerin Society became a key vehicle for the development and promulgation of neoliberal ideas, which were spread via an informal network of think tanks, journalists and academics. This was a successful tactic and the key themes of neoliberalism – the efficiency of the market, the inefficiency of government and individualism – became embedded in popular discourse. Individualism is a key trope of all forms of liberalism. However, in neoliberalism, there is a zealous commitment to its pursuit. This can be seen in the celebration of success and excess. In the fields of welfare and penal policy, it manifests itself in terms of debates about individual responsibility.

Neoliberalism presents itself as bringing Adam Smith's insights on the efficacy of the market to the modern economic system (Leyva, 2018). One of the most prominent and influential right-wing think tanks is the Adam Smith Institute. Neoliberal political philosophy argues that the whole of society should be viewed as a competitive market arena. In the political context of the late 1970s, this meant that the state had become too big and powerful. There was one exception to this – law and order – where Thatcher and others argued that the state had become weak and ineffectual. The model of homo economicus assumes that we will only behave ethically and altruistically if we benefit personally. One of the key areas for political philosophy is the problem of distributive justice. Here, the question is how the state should distribute burdens and benefits among citizens. Nozick (1974) identifies two theories of distributive justice: patterned and historical. A patterned theory states that a distribution is just only if it satisfies a certain pattern. However, this will inevitably involve greater involvement by the state and thereby restrict freedom, and is therefore unjust (Nozick, 1974). Nozick acknowledges that liberty and equality are always in tension, but as liberty is the supreme political value, these concerns trump others.

Nozick (1974) put forward a thought experiment involving the famous basketball player Walt Chamberlain. He will play only if, in addition to his normal salary, 25c from the price of each ticket of admission goes to him. Over one season, 1 million people come to see Chamberlain play and happily drop 25c into a special box with his name on it. Nozick (1974) argues that the only way we can return to the pattern is by interfering with either the freedom of individuals to choose how they will exercise their talents, or the freedom of individuals to choose how to spend money to which they are entitled. The thought experiment is also an example of the functioning of the market: Chamberlin has freely negotiated the contract; and the people who pay the 25c to him choose to do so.

The neoliberal claim to be updating or applying Smith to the late 20th century ignores key aspects of his arguments (Leyva, 2018). The homo economicus model is based on a notion derived from Smith that human beings are essentially selfish. However, in his often-neglected

The Theory of Moral Sentiments, originally published in 1796, Smith (2010) acknowledged that, as is clearly the case, human beings also have the potential for compassion, empathy and altruism. Smith was also in favour of public education and government policies to improve the conditions of the working class. Given the development of the huge corporations that has been such a feature of the neoliberal era, it is significant that Smith was also opposed to concentrations of power. Leyva (2018) notes that Smith presents a model that is rather at odds with the modern interpretation of his ideas. It is based on small enterprises that avoid repetitive and alienating work, and capital needs to be securely located in the community so that it can be aware of the impact of industrial development. By marketising and monetising as many aspects of life as possible, neoliberalism inevitably leads to a politics that rejects liberal and progressive ideas.

Against welfare

In the period that this volume covers, welfare policy has been heavily influenced by key New Right thinkers, particularly Hayek and Friedman. The expansion in imprisonment has occurred alongside attacks on the welfare state. The charge against the welfare state is that it is expensive and produces dependency. Part of this 'war of position' (Gramsci, 1971) has been the demonisation of the poor and those who are in receipt of benefits. Welshman (2013) demonstrates that this is not a new phenomenon. However, in the age of mass media, it has become increasingly virulent and powerful. Politicians from Thatcher onwards have presented welfare recipients as a group who are 'other'. In addition, the political discourse is now full of terms such as 'hard-working families' or 'strivers versus shirkers'. This discourse is based on a form of binary opposition. It ignores the fact that the welfare state is complex, with individuals and families across society benefiting at various points (Hills, 2017). However, the 'them versus us' rhetoric is deeply embedded.

One of the major shifts that have occurred in British society since 1979 has been an increase in inequality. The argument put forward by Hayek (2014) is that any attempts to interfere with the dynamics of the market are doomed to fail. From this perspective, inequality is a fact of life. Skills and abilities are not distributed evenly and the market reflects the value that society places on them. Inequality is also viewed as producing the competitive dynamism that market economies require. One of the attacks on the welfare state is that it stifles enterprise as it leads to higher levels of personal taxation. Before the banking crisis of 2008, inequality in the UK had been increasing (Dorling et al, 2007); however, the policy of austerity has made these trends worse (Cummins, 2018).

The UN special rapporteur's report on poverty in the UK (Alston, 2018) outlined the impact of austerity measures. The report concluded that 14 million people in the UK – a fifth of the population – live in poverty. This figure was based on a new measure of poverty that takes into account costs such as housing and childcare. It concluded that the UK's social safety net had been removed as the result of deliberate policy decisions based on ideological considerations. The report was highly critical of the Universal Credit (UC) system. Not only is there a five-week gap before any payments are made, but claims for UC are also made online, which assumes that claimants have Internet access. However, the poorest in society are both most likely to claim UC and least likely to have easy Internet access. Alston (2018) suggested that the result was 'a digital and sanitised version of the 19th Century workhouse, made infamous by Charles Dickens'.

The cultural shift towards individualism has involved not only the celebration of success, but also the denigration of so-called 'failure'. Mass media has a critical role in defining the most important issues of the day, as well as the parameters within which they are discussed (Hall, 1997). This is particularly the case in the area of welfare policy. The term 'welfare' is increasingly constructed in negative ways (Garrett, 2017), which has a very important impact, including on what is actually seen as welfare. In modern debates, the term is constructed in such a way as to exclude pensions – the biggest section of the welfare budget. Jensen and Tyler (2015) argue that the media, particularly the tabloid press and reality TV (RT) programmes, have had a key role in shaping what they term 'anti-welfare common sense'. There has always been a stigma attached to living in poverty. Stigma is relational (Goffman, 2009), in that it shapes our interactions as well as our attitudes. The result is that the stigmatised attribute, in this case, living in poverty, moves that individual from 'a whole and usual to a discounted one' (Goffman, 2009). Tyler (2018a) is critical of the essentially apolitical approach that Goffman (2009) adopted. She argues that the focus on the relational nature of stigma ignores the structural issues that underpin it and the political heavy lifting that it does. Tyler (2018a) argues that Goffman (2009) ignores the political implications of the role that stigma has in shaping political discourse and debate.

The anti-welfare discourse that portrays the welfare state as overgenerous and creating dependency feeds into attitudes towards those who are in receipt of benefits. Populist politicians can then make claims that are based on these notions. Reagan's infamous 'welfare queens' campaign speeches are an example of this. At campaign rallies, Reagan made a series of claims about fraud within the welfare system. As well as being anti-welfare, these were highly racialised. They played to two deeply engrained sexist and racist tropes about African-Americans: uncontrolled sexuality and laziness (Gilliam, 1999). The merging of these gendered, racialised and anti-welfare discourses reinforces racist and sexist stereotypes while undermining wider public support for anti-poverty programmes (Cammett, 2014).

Lakoff and Johnson (1980) conclude that people in power impose their metaphors on wider society. The metaphors and myths of welfare have important consequences, for example, Hills (2015) notes that the public consistently overestimate what percentage of the welfare state budget is spent on out-of-work benefits. In a 2012 survey on this issue, respondents were informed that the 'government's welfare budget pays for pensions, tax credits, benefits for the unemployed, the disabled and other groups'. When asked 'Out of every £100 of this welfare budget, how much do you think is spent on benefits for unemployed people?', 50 per cent of respondents answered that 40 per cent or more was spent on the unemployed, with 25 per cent answering more than 60 per cent. However, the actual figure is 4 per cent (Hills, 2015). Similarly, there are huge overestimates for the extent of fraudulent claims for benefits. The Department for Work and Pensions (DWP) estimated that 0.7 per cent of all benefits are overpaid as the result of fraud. For Jobseeker's Allowance, the figure was 2.9 per cent. However, when asked about fraud, the average estimate by the public was 27 per cent (Hills, 2015).

The preceding discussion highlights the influence that misconceptions of the welfare state can have. Alongside this is the view that the welfare state creates dependency and 'rewards' anti-social behaviour. Jensen and Tyler (2015) view this as a form of political economy, which they call a hardening of 'anti-welfare common-sense'. The tabloid media and RT programmes have had a key role to play in these developments. There is a whole range of RT programmes that claim to give an insight into the daily life of the communities and individuals that take part. There is a subsection of the genre that looks at the lives of the rich, for example, *Made in Chelsea* or *The Real Housewives of Cheshire*. These programmes emphasise the wealth and conspicuous consumption of the young and perma-tanned. One of the interesting subtexts of these programmes is that behind all the shallow glamour, the featured individuals are really like the rest of the population struggling with the demands of modern life. One of these struggles is, ironically, maintaining the status in the celebrity firmament. This form of RT allows the viewer a glimpse into a world that is out of reach to all those but the extremely wealthy. The clear message is that this is a world that we should aspire to be part of: if we work hard enough, the market will provide sufficient rewards to fund such a lifestyle.

The gaze of *The Real Housewives of Cheshire* is upwards and envious. This can be contrasted with the gaze of another subsection of the RT genre: so-called 'poverty porn'. The gaze of poverty porn is downward and disparaging. The best example of poverty porn is *Benefits Street*. The programme claimed to show what life was really like in one street in a deprived area of Birmingham. The title is disingenuous as not everyone living in the street or featured in the programme is in receipt of benefits. The programme was actually filmed in James Turner Street in Birmingham. This distortion of the nature and extent of welfare is part of the attack upon it (Garland, 2014). The programme opens with a shot of a litter-strewn street and then focuses on a drug dealer, Maxwell. It is later revealed that Maxwell is in prison, thereby the programme conflates welfare with crime. Crossley (2017) emphasises the way that the media representation of those living in poverty produces disgust at individuals and areas. It does not focus on the underlying structural issues that result in poverty. For RT programmes such as *Benefits Street*, the starting point appears to be an uncritical acceptance of Murray's (1990) notion of the underclass. Murray presents the underclass as being socially, physically and psychologically cut off from mainstream society (Cummins, 2016a). Murray places the blame for this solely at the door of an overgenerous and indulgent welfare state. Thus, the issue becomes welfare dependency, not poverty (Peck and Theodore, 2010).

One of the key mythologies of the overly generous welfare state is that allows 'excessive breeding'. Jensen and Tyler (2015) use the term 'benefits brood' to capture the way that families with large numbers of children feature in the tabloid press. These debates start from an implicit assumption that there is an agreement on what constitutes a large family. In April 2017, a two-child policy in benefits was introduced. The policy means that if a family claims child tax credit or UC and has a third child born after 6 April 2017, they will be unable to claim increased benefits. Such a claim would be worth up to £2,780 a year. Perkins (2016), inspired by Eysenck, put forward the proposition that the welfare state provides incentives for the least capable (that is, the poorest) parents to have more children. Caspi et al (2016) argued that it was possible to identify future criminals and those who will place the greatest demand on welfare services by means of a simple test at the age of three. While this is junk science it should be noted that being in receipt of welfare and criminality are used almost interchangeably.

As well as highlighting unusual cases of large families, the tabloid media focus on welfare fraud and crimes committed by those on benefits. High-profile media cases, which, by definition, are unusual, are used as somehow being representative of all families on benefits. Jensen and Tyler (2015) discuss the Philpott case as an example of these processes. Mick Philpott was the father of 17 children. He planned an arson attack at his home that led to the death of six of his children. Just as Nelson (2014) claimed that *Benefits Street* lifted the lid on what he termed 'Britain's dirty secret', he suggested that the Philpott case was a direct result of the welfare state. Jensen and Tyler (2015) note that Philpott had actually appeared on RT. This helps to create the impression that there are more families such as his than actually exist. *The Sun* submitted a freedom of information request to the DWP in 2012. It was probably disappointed when the reply indicated that there were ten families dependent on benefits in which there were 13 or more children. Here, the issue is not to try and excuse in any way the awful crimes that Mick Philpott committed; rather, it is to refute any suggestion that the case can be seen as representative in any meaningful sense.

Stigma operates on both several levels. If, as Goffman (2009) does, we limit our analysis to interpersonal relations, we are ignoring the political economy of stigma (Tyler, 2018b). One of the impacts of the social and economic policies that have been followed since 1979 has been the spatial concentration of poverty, particularly in urban areas (Wacquant, 2008, 2009a, 2009b). Wacquant (2007) uses the term 'advanced marginality' as a way of capturing this spatial concentration, as well as the way that it cuts communities off from the wider society. Davis (2006), in his path-breaking study of Los Angeles, outlined the way that the development of modern cities means that there are areas that effectively exclude the poor. These developments have to be linked to the labour market. Precarity extends from work to housing and accommodation, and vice versa. Wacquant (2007) describes territorial stigmatisation as the outcome of processes whereby areas become marginalised. The wider area then stigmatises individuals who live in those areas. McKenzie (2015), in her ethnographic study of the St Ann's estate in Nottingham, shows that the wider society stigmatises its residents in a number of ways. This is a further example of the process whereby poverty becomes viewed as an issue of individual moral weakness rather than structural inequalities. Wacquant (2007: 66–7) argues that areas subject to territorial stigmatisation experience:

> forms of poverty that are neither residual, nor cyclical or transitional, but inscribed in the future of contemporary societies insofar as they are fed by the ongoing fragmentation of the wage relationship, the functional disconnection of dispossessed neighbourhoods from the national and global economies, and the reconfiguration of the welfare state in the polarizing city.

In popular and policy discourse, the areas that Wacquant describes are often referred to as 'sink estates'. The term actually comes from a series of experiments on rats carried out by the ethologist John B Calhoun in the late 1950s. Calhoun and his colleagues carried out a series of experiments in what they termed 'rat utopias'. The rats were given access to unlimited food and water, which led to uncontrolled population growth. In his report of the experiments and the social collapse that resulted from overcrowding, Calhoun used the term 'behavioural sink'. Calhoun's work became hugely influential but it was used in a way that went counter to his intentions (Ramsden and Adams, 2009). In his analysis of the roots and spread of this term, Slater (2018) shows that it has become a term that is used to encapsulate, from the perspectives of politicians and policymakers, all the problems of advanced marginality. It is used almost as if it is an analytical term but it is really a pejorative term that has no real analytical value. It has been used by journalists, free market think tanks and politicians to push for a particular model of urban redevelopment. Slater (2018) notes the huge symbolism of Blair giving his first speech as Prime Minister on the Aylesbury Estate in South London, using rhetoric that was not that far removed from Murray, to talk of the underclass. Slater (2018) notes that the sink estate discourse reverses causality: people access social housing because they cannot afford to buy or rent privately; social housing itself does not make people poor. Alongside this, the sink estate discourse carries with it a series of assumptions. These include the fact that sink estates allegedly create poverty, intergenerational worklessness, welfare dependency and crime. The fact that the term 'sink estate' has its roots in an experiment regarding animal behaviour means that it has explicit eugenicist overtones.

Conclusion

Fukuyama (1992) presents the triumph of free market economics as an inevitable conclusion of trends in human history. It is also presented as the final stage in which development has ceased or is complete. Even in 1992, many doubted this claim. The rise of populism, the climate crisis and ongoing conflicts that lead to refugee crises seem to make Fukuyama's claims even weaker. History has certainly not ended and liberal democracy does not seem anywhere as secure as he imagined. Fukuyama (2018) argued that liberal democracy had shakier foundations. However, he identified the threats to liberal democracies not as the rise of populism and nationalism, but rather as coming from what he terms 'identity politics'. There is a huge irony in this volte-face. Fukuyama (2018) uses the term 'identity politics' to cover social and civil rights movements that seek legal and political equality for women and sexual and racial minorities. The roots of these progressive political movements can be found in certain iterations of liberalism.

Brown (2015) provides an analysis of the contemporary forms of neoliberalism. At its core, is what Brown (2015) terms the 'financialisation of everything'. This excludes other more pro-social concepts such as community, the social good or mutuality. Neoliberalism has resulted in the outsourcing of key functions of the state. Brown notes that neoliberalism requires not only the introduction of market mechanisms to state functions, but also the transformation of state agencies into firms. In the crash of 2008, the banks were described as 'too big to fail'. As Brown argues, the corollary of this is that some are 'too small to protect'. In his analysis of neoliberalism, Foucault (2008) concludes that everyone is imagined as human capital.

Giroux (2011) sums up neoliberalism as an attack on the welfare state, which has seen the shredding of the social contract that was central to post-war liberal democracies. These processes have seen the market and market values pushing out notions of solidarity, economic justice and the common good. These are, of course, at the heart of debates about welfare and penal policy.

Somers (2008) produces a 'triadic' model of society, with the three elements being the state, the market and civil society. Her analysis describes neoliberalism as a form of 'market fundamentalism'. Market fundamentalism sees civil society as a potential barrier to the implementation and functioning of market mechanisms. Somers (2008) argues that neoliberalism has a deeply corrosive impact on citizenship, and concludes that market fundamentalism has led to increasing numbers of people having lost any meaningful membership of civil society. Citizenship has become contractualised and commodified.

Somers's (2008) model requires a balance between the state, market and civil society for individuals to be regarded as socially included citizens. In this model of a balance of powers between the three elements, civil society can act as a bulwark to protect individuals against the excesses of both the state and the market. Wright (1997) argues that this spatial representation is in danger of ignoring or simplifying the way that in modern capitalist societies, the market, state and civil society are connected and enmeshed in many complex ways. Far from seeing the rolling back of the state, neoliberalism has actually seen its retooling (Peck and Theodore, 2010).

Polanyi (1957) was highly critical of those committed to a free market model. He described the notion of a self-regulating global system as a 'stark utopia'. Polanyi's (1957) use of the term 'utopia' here is deliberate: progressive politics are often attacked from the Right for being utopian. In particular, progressive ideas are seen as running counter to the selfishness of homo economicus. Polanyi saw the seductive attraction of arguments that would see the state and the role of politics diminish. He countered these arguments as follows. The government did not interfere in the economy; rather, it was an integral part of it. Economies would not function without government activity. Free market rhetoric hides the fact that government secures the conditions that allow businesses to profit. Increasingly, in the areas of welfare and penal policies, the state is the source of those profits. Polanyi asserts the primacy of politics. Thus, it is impossible to separate economic and political development. The prosperity of the post-war period can thus be viewed as a direct result of the advances in politics and civil society that occurred in the period.

Since the election of Margaret Thatcher in 1979, economic as well as social policy has been cast in her shadow. One of the undoubted impacts of her electoral success was to move the political centre in UK politics to the right. Thatcher herself was wedded to traditional Tory social and family values. She combined these with a commitment to a belief in the 'free market'. Alongside this, she had a suspicious and hostile attitude towards the welfare state. There are significant differences between the Thatcher, Major, New Labour and Cameron administrations. These are discussed in subsequent chapters. However, I think it is possible to identify these trace elements in the development of penal and welfare policy. These elements include a belief that the welfare state is monolithic, produces dependency and rewards or actively encourages anti-social behaviour. All these administrations oversaw expansions in the use of imprisonment. As well as a dominant economic discourse, there was a dominant one in welfare and penal policy.

3

Contemporary Narratives of Mass Incarceration

Introduction

This chapter will explore contemporary narratives of the expansion of the use of imprisonment, with a focus on the experiences of the US and England and Wales. Lloyd and Whitehead (2018) argue that the development and growth of mass incarceration are endogenous features of neoliberalism. The term 'mass incarceration' is used here to donate the expansion of the use of imprisonment that has occurred across a number of jurisdictions since the early 1980s (Simon, 2007). The US is the country where the rise in the use of imprisonment has been most dramatic. Lloyd and Whitehead (2018) conclude that there is a distinctive form of neoliberal penality that has developed over the past 40 years. This chapter argues that this approach offers a partial explanation. To begin with, we need to examine the term 'neoliberalism', which has become such a dominant one in the analysis of modern social policy. The extensive use of the term generates its own difficulties (Garrett, 2019). For some, the term is used so broadly to describe such a range of social, economic and political policies that it has lost its original, theoretical, conceptual and analytical value.

Venugopal (2015) is particularly critical of the way that term 'neoliberalism' has been so widely and loosely used. He notes that 'There were just 103 Google Scholar entries in English with the term "neoliberal" or "neoliberalism" in the title between 1980 and 1989. This had multiplied to 1,324 for 1990–9, and 7,138 for 2000–9' (Venugopal, 2015: 165–6). The electoral successes of politicians influenced by Hayek (2014), Friedman (2009) and the Chicago School led to neoliberalism becoming a term that was both 'omnipresent' and 'promiscuous' (Clarke, 2008: 135). Garrett (2019) notes that critics suggest that neoliberalism has become a meta-narrative. 'Neoliberal' has become such an elastic term that it is applied across a range of political and economic settings. Dunn (2017) notes that the term has most traction in academia and among 'left elites'. Other writers have continued to find the term useful as an analytical tool. Bourdieu (2001) saw neoliberalism as a 'conservative revolution' that sought to overthrow the post-war social-democratic consensus. This aim has largely been achieved.

Neoliberalism and mass incarceration

The key features of neoliberalism are well documented. These include attempts to expand the so-called mechanisms of the market to all areas of life, for example, through the monetisation of human activity and relationships (Harvey, 2005; Brown, 2015, 2019). On its own terms, neoliberalism is committed to a small state and personal freedom. As Lloyd and Whitehead (2018) note, this notion of the small state does not apply in the area of penal policy, with the US and the UK, in particular, having seen huge increases in the numbers of those subject to imprisonment. Neoliberalism is a cultural and social, as well as an economic and political, phenomenon (Giroux, 2011). In the cultural and social field, Bauman (2008) outlines what he termed a culture of 'hyperindividualism', which leads to a loosening and weakening of social and community ties. The various forms of neoliberalism share a commitment to a small state – apart from the area of law and order. This has led to the expansion of the market or market mechanisms into a range of areas that were previously seen as the realm or the sole responsibility of the state. The penal field is one area that has seen a number of such developments, including the establishment of private prisons, the privatisation of the probation service in England and Wales, and the outsourcing of other functions, such as the electronic tagging of offenders (Cummins, 2016b). Fraser (2016), in her analysis of the rise of Trump and the Brexit vote, argued that these shifts marked the end of what she termed 'progressive neoliberalism'. For Fraser (2016), 'progressive neoliberalism' represents an unholy alliance between social progressive values in the areas of gender and race, for example, and neoliberal economics. The Clinton and the later Blair administrations represent the two best examples of Fraser's progressive neoliberalism.

Lloyd and Whitehead (2018) argue that as an economic and political phenomenon, neoliberalism provides a necessary and sufficient explanation for the development of mass incarceration. Support for this analytical approach can be found in the work of Wacquant (2008, 2009a, 2009b, 2012). Wacquant argued that the key premises of neoliberalism have been accepted by parties of both the Left and the Right. In the penal field, the result has been that the key *doxa* of the penal state, such as 'prison works', zero tolerance and broken windows policing, have been widely accepted, until relatively recently, in an uncritical fashion. The overall outcome has termed the 'decline of the rehabilitative ideal' (Garland, 2001). The CJS and other systems focus on the management of risk (Beck, 1992; Webb, 2006). Offenders are now regarded as sites of risk rather than marginalised individuals in need of social and welfare support to be reintegrated into wider society. The act of imprisonment is an act of state violence, and alongside the impact on individuals, communities and families, it has huge symbolic significance and value.

The rise in the use of imprisonment has been termed 'mass incarceration' and the development of the 'penal state'. It has been one of the most significant social and public policy developments of the past 40 years. It has taken place in a number of jurisdictions, though is most apparent in the US, which has seen the development of a huge prison–industrial complex. There are now over 2 million people in US jails. An oft-quoted statistic is that while the US has 5 per cent of the world's population, it has over 25 per cent of the world's prisoners. In Europe, England and Wales have followed this trend most closely. The expansion of the penal state has occurred over a prolonged period. However, during the period since the early 1980s, it is clear that governments in both the US and the UK have followed market-oriented policies, sought to reduce the welfare state and largely accepted the notion that prison acts as a deterrent to offending. Free market economics were, on the whole, combined with tougher law-and-order approaches. The political success of Reagan and Thatcher meant that there was a rightwards shift in debates about law and order (Simon, 2007). Parties nominally of the Left or Centre-Left moved to the right on these issues, fearing that they would be portrayed as weak on crime or as 'on the side of the offender'.

Lloyd and Whitehead (2018) view the causes as ultimately the result of neoliberal economic policies. In this model, mass incarceration becomes a way of managing the urban poor. This approach, the authors note, is influenced by the work of scholars such as Wacquant (2008, 2009a, 2009b, 2012). There are limitations with this approach, not the least of which is transporting an analysis so heavily grounded in the US experience and applying it to the UK and across other jurisdictions. There may well be many similarities, for example, it is clear that much of the New Labour discourse on rights and responsibilities was adopted almost wholesale from Clinton's Democrats. However, as Garland (2018) notes, it is impossible to talk of one US experience of mass incarceration because of the differences between the 50 states. When comparing penal regimes, it is important to take account of a range of factors. Lacey (2008) argues that liberal market economies have more deeply established notions of individualism, and that this is one factor in more punitive approaches to penal policy. Cavadino and Dignan (2006) developed a political-economy typology of penal regimes: neoliberal, conservative-corporatist, social-democratic and oriental-corporatist. A focus on economic factors alone becomes reductionist and potentially excludes important factors in any analysis. In addition, an economic base–superstructure model of penality overlooks the importance of broader social, political and cultural shifts, which all have a huge potential impact on penal policy. Hall et al (2013) emphasise the need to develop an analysis of cultural values in mapping the shifts in penal policy as while economic issues are clearly vitally important, they cannot tell the whole story.

Garland (2004) argues that increasingly punitive attitudes reflect social dislocation and the 'othering' of social groups – in this case, the marginalised urban poor and those from minority communities. Modern approaches to punishment and broader penal policy create an image of the offender as an outsider – someone who by the virtue of committing crime, has surrendered future liberty claims. These attitudes underpin the call for 'tougher' punishments, longer sentences and harsher conditions in prisons. In Becker's (1968) model, offenders are making a rational choice to commit crime. Possible punishment or other sanctions are part of a cost–benefit analysis that offenders make; thus, harsher punishment will change the nature of these decisions. A more traditional welfare approach sees the roots of offending in personal and social circumstances. A more individualistic society has seen crime become seen much more as an issue of personal responsibility. Garrett (2015) argues that crime is now seen as the result of the lack of individual and social control. In the politics of law and order, populist politicians make direct appeals to voters over the need to be tougher on crime. In making these appeals, liberal elites – policymakers and academics – are presented as weak and ineffectual, being more concerned with the human rights of offenders than the impact of crime. Hall et al (2013) highlight the powerful role that such appeals have. Hall (1979) showed that in making a series of calls to 'ordinary citizens', Thatcher effectively exploited law-and-order concerns in her development of populist authoritarianism. In the UK, no politician has been able to shift the debates back to the centre ground since. In his early days as Prime Minister, Boris Johnson and his Home Secretary, Priti Patel, made a series of policy announcement, such as increasing the number of police officers and restricting the early release of offenders committed of violent and sexual offences. These moves were strong echoes of the 'get tough' law-and-order Conservative Party policies of the late 1970s and early 1980s.

Mass incarceration in the US

The development of mass incarceration in the US stands apart in its scale. However, that does not mean that there are not vital lessons for other countries. Simon (2014) compared the expansion of the use of imprisonment to a biblical flood – a flood that he now sees as past its peak – and identifies three elements or phases in the development of mass incarceration. First, driven by a fear of crime and the political fallout from being seen as weak on the issue (Simon, 2007), prosecutors ask for custodial sentences where previously a community penalty would have been imposed. Then, sentences are increased. Finally, mandatory and or indeterminate sentences are introduced. Garland (2018) argues that while broad explanations of the sort that are offered by meta-narratives, such as neoliberal penality or a new Jim Crow, provided the initial theoretical explanations for the rise of mass incarceration, they have been challenged by more fine-grained analyses that highlight the complex range of local and other factors. He concludes that:

> The institutional terrain upon which 'mass incarceration' was built turns out to be quite varied, as are local penal politics. And although all 50 states and the federal government have increased incarceration, there have been marked differences in the kinds of transformations that have occurred, both quantitatively and qualitatively; and the multiple processes driving prison growth need to be specified and disaggregated.
>
> (Garland, 2018: 23)

As Garland (2018) notes, the Californian experience is very different to that of the state of Maine. The three-strikes law is often quoted as one of the drivers of increased incarceration rates across the US. However, the particular way that the law was operated in California led to very significant rises in incarceration rates that did not occur in other states where it was introduced in a different fashion (Zimring et al, 2001). The large-scale narratives of mass incarceration provide many insights and open up theoretical explanations but they also obscure local and other factors that provide a more complete picture. This is as true for nations as it is for the individual states of the US.

One of the key questions to consider in response to Lloyd and Whitehead is whether it is possible to identify a distinctive neoliberal penality. The starting point for this has to be an examination of neoliberalism. The analysis of neoliberalism has concentrated on two very broad areas (Wacquant, 2012). The first is essentially an economic model that examines the application of the market and market forces to areas of public and private life that were previously seen as 'social goods' or 'beyond the market'. Under the Thatcher government in the UK, this model was followed in social housing, public utilities and a number of other areas. It has since been extended to the penal system and wider aspects of the CJS. Harvey (2005) has described this process as 'accumulation by dispossession'.

Nozick (1974) emphasises the role that the state has in securing and maintaining the liberty of the subject. Thus, the expansion of what he termed the 'nightwatchman state' is not necessarily inconsistent. From this perspective, increasingly punitive social and penal policies and the expansion of the penal state fit with a schema that it is argued enhance individual liberty. The second but linked perspective is influenced by Foucault's notion of governmentality. These approaches examine the way that power has become decentralised in late-modern capitalist society. This has created a discourse of self-government and regulation as the defining features of citizenship. Foucault (2008) examines the construction of the modern discourse of citizenship, with its emphasis on self-government. In this schema, neoliberalism is characterised as a shift in the relationship between the individual and the state, with the goal of the state therefore being to produce self-regulating citizens.

Wacquant (2012: 66) argues that these two broad approaches 'obscure what is neo about neo-liberalism': it is a political project that involves the dismantling of welfare provisions. 'Workfare' or 'prisonfare' are the new means of regulating marginal urban populations. These processes involve a rebalancing of what Bourdieu termed the left and right hands of the state. For Bourdieu, the left hand of the state represents what would be very broadly termed 'social welfare', that is, education, health and social work; the right hand is the police, courts and penal system. Wacquant (2012) describes the shift as a move from the protective (feminine and collectivising) to the disciplinary (masculine and individualising). This notion of the state has been criticised for its binary nature as it fails to recognise that agencies on both sides perform what can be broadly termed disciplinary and welfare roles (Garrett, 2007).

Wacquant's (2008, 2009a, 2009b, 2012) work provides an analysis of the development of more punitive welfare and penal policies, seeing them as integral features of the neoliberal political project. He acknowledges that these shifts are not simply about changes in government and public policy; rather, neoliberalism adopts what Gramsci (1971) terms a 'war of position' against the welfare state. In this war of position, think tanks, academics and sympathetic journalists have had a key role in the spreading of the *doxa* of neoliberalism and the penal state. Wacquant uses the term '*doxa*' to mean the terms that set the parameters of a debate or phrases that are commonly used but never properly interrogated. In the economic and social spheres, these would include 'market', 'flexibility', 'choice' and 'individualism'. In the penal sphere, phrases such as 'prison works', 'zero tolerance' and 'broken windows' have all become *doxa* (Wacquant, 2008, 2009a, 2009b). Wacquant (2008) concludes that the penal system under neoliberalism has become a key state function that manages, but also produces, inequality.

One of the difficulties with Wacquant's thesis – and the one presented by Lloyd and Whitehead here – is the deterministic and mechanistic link between the rise in rates of imprisonment and the rise of the influence of neoliberal ideas. This minimises the other factors that are potentially at play, for example, the influence of a high-profile case or a moral panic about a particular sort of crime. It is also dependent on a rather monolithic view of governments, failing to recognise the often apparently contradictory policy positions that are adopted. For example, in the UK, in the late 1980s and early 1990s, the Home Office under a liberal Home Secretary, Douglas Hurd, sought to introduce a range of community-based alternatives to imprisonment, all based on the premise that 'prison is an expensive way of making bad people worse' (Gottschalk, 2006).

As Hall (1979) pointed out, Thatcherism was a mixture of free market economics and traditional Conservative social values. These are not necessarily always in alignment. In this case, we can see that there is a tension between different areas of government. When Hurd became Foreign Secretary, he was succeeded by the right-wing populist David Waddington. After the demise of Thatcher, it was the appointment of another populist, Michael Howard, as Home Secretary in 1991 that marked the rapid expansion of the use of imprisonment in England and Wales. As he announced at the Conservative Party conference in 1991,

Howard was committed to a penal philosophy based on the notion that 'prison works'. In England and Wales, the rate of incarceration increased following this, as well as in the New Labour years (1997–2010). In the period between June 1993 and June 2012, the prison population in England and Wales increased by 41,800 to over 86,000 (Ministry of Justice, 2014).

There is a huge debate about the nature of New Labour but, certainly in the period 1997–2005, it oversaw significant investment in health and social welfare programmes such as Sure Start. The contrast with the current position of welfare systems, as outlined in the UN rapporteur's report (Alston, 2018), could not be starker. Yet, the rate of the use of imprisonment continued to rise. However New Labour is characterised, its investment in education, health and other areas is very much at odds with the principles of Hayek (2014) and Friedman (2009). There is something of a parallel here with Hinton's (2016) analysis of the Johnson administration, in which progressive social policies combined with increasingly punitive penal and welfare policies. The growth in the use of imprisonment in the UK and US continued under Clinton and Blair, who led nominally progressive parties (Wacquant, 2009a, 2009b). Alongside the rise in the use of imprisonment, New Labour's communitarian-influenced wider social policy saw the introduction of a raft of measures imposing societal norms on the marginalised, such as Anti-Social Behaviour Orders (ASBOs) (Butler and Drakeford, 2001).

Race and mass incarceration

The USA's history of slavery, racial segregation and discrimination forms the historical backdrop to Wacquant's analysis of the modern penal system. Wacquant (2002) produced an analysis of the modalities of racial oppression in the US. They are clearly interlinked and, in this sense, one can draw a line from slavery to mass incarceration. However, it is not a direct parallel as presented in the Lloyd and Whitehead model. These modalities of oppression share a set of racist beliefs but they function in quite different ways.

The historical and ongoing over-representation of African-Americans in the CJS is well documented (Wacquant, 2009a; Drucker, 2011; Alexander, 2012; Hinton, 2018). There are some elements of US exceptionalism at play here. However, it would be a mistake to assume that these issues do not arise in other penal systems. The Lammy Inquiry (Lammy, 2017) highlighted the impact of racism on the experiences of particularly young black men in the UK system.

There is a significant literature that highlights the impact of increasingly punitive law and order policies on the African-American community. The combination of neoliberal economic policies, the rise of the penal state and legacies of slavery, Jim Crow, and other forms of racist exclusion have led to the current position. Hinton (2018) notes that, in recent years, the gulf between incarceration rates for black people and white people have narrowed. The statistics remain shocking:

- black men represent 13 per cent of the US male population but 35 per cent of all men serving state or federal sentences of more than a year;
- one in three black men born in 2001 can expect to be incarcerated at some point in their lifetime compared to one in 17 white men;
- one in 18 black women born in 2001 will be incarcerated compared to one in 45 Latina women and one in 111 white women.

These figures are not some contemporary aberration; they are the result of historical and contemporary racist processes that have targeted the black community. The backdrop to these CJS figures is the deeply entrenched racist nature of US society that sees African-Americans experiencing levels of extreme poverty, economic and educational disadvantage, poor housing, and other factors that contribute to crime. In addition, the African-American community experiences over-policing and a concomitant lack of protection (Brown, 2004; Brunson and Miller, 2005; Owusu-Bempah, 2017; Baldwin, 2018).

Mass incarceration has not solely been driven by racist ideas, but the centrality of their role has to be examined. The 13th Amendment abolished slavery but there is an exception for those convicted of a crime. Blackmon (2008) shows that this loophole was used to target newly emancipated former slaves. Following the end of the Civil War, states in the former Confederacy enacted a series of laws that became known as the Black Codes. These laws meant that emancipated slaves were denied the rights of full citizenship, for example, the right to vote or serve on juries. At the same time, the use of vagrancy laws meant that any black person who could not prove that they were employed could be arrested. The convict-leasing system meant that private employers could then use the labour of the incarcerated. Blackmon (2008) shows the key role that the convict-leasing system had in key areas, for example, on former plantations, as well as mining and railways. He shows that, for example, the rates of arrest for 'vagrancy' offences increased in line with seasonal demands for labour. These arrests were made on the basis of no real evidence and often simply amounted to the rounding up of poor black men. In Northern states, the CJS was also used as a means of surveillance and control of black communities. The outcome of these two strategies was the incarceration of black people at higher rates. This then became the basis for a series of racist tropes about the alleged nature of black criminality that remain deeply engrained within US political debates. Haney-López (2014) has explored the way that politicians can exploit these by making dog-whistle calls to voters, that is, using coded language or phrases that appeal to racist tropes without using racist terms. Trump has done this on numerous occasions, though he does not exactly blow a dog whistle as use a racist megaphone.

The historical and contemporary over-representation of African-Americans in the CJS is thus based on a range of wider social, economic and political factors. However, as Muhammed (2010) notes, the high arrest and incarceration rates have led to what he terms a 'statistical discourse'. In this discourse, the factors that lead to higher arrest and incarceration rates are ignored. The rates themselves are used to inform political and popular debates, which then shift the focus from the historic legacy of slavery and modern structural factors to the so-called failings of the African-American family, for example, the absence of male role models. There is an explicit link between welfare and penal policy here. Attacks on the welfare state from the Right have focused on its alleged profligacy, creation of dependency and extent of fraud within the system. Anti-welfare on the Right has been linked with racist and anti-immigrant discourses (Cummins, 2018). Murray's (1990, 1994, 2012) notion of the underclass is constructed in largely racist terms. In his attacks on the role of the welfare state, Meade (1992) does so in dog-whistle terms. Reagan's political use of the 'welfare queen' and the media reporting of it referenced deeply entrenched constructions of black female sexuality (Kohler-Hausmann, 2015). In the 1988 presidential election, the George Bush Sr Willie Horton attack ad on Dukakis played on series of stereotypes of the dangers posed by black male sexuality that can be traced back to slavery (Saul, 2017).

Alexander (2012) argues that mass incarceration and the policies linked to it have created a new caste of socially excluded young African-American males. This includes those who are incarcerated as well as formerly incarcerated individuals, who are denied the full rights of citizenship – including often the right to vote – and who struggle to find employment. Alexander (2012) concludes that these developments have put the gains of the Civil Rights era under pressure. There is a similar pattern to the post- Civil War period, where the CJS and policing undermine political and social progress. Laws are not written in the explicitly racist fashion of the late 19th century; however, Hinton (2018) demonstrates that laws that are, at face value, racially neutral impact disproportionately on black people. The most important example of this is the wider 'war on drugs'. For example, policies such as drug-free zones and habitual offender laws have a greater impact on African-Americans. Those convicted of selling drugs within drug-free zones close to protected areas, for example, schools or parks, face increased sentences. Alongside other factors, the impact of policies of segregation in housing means that such policies impact disproportionately on African-American communities. Other policies, such as zero tolerance and broken windows policing, which focus on low-level quality-of-life crimes in the belief that such crimes lead to more major crimes, have become key features of modern social and penal policy. They also lead to the targeting of police resources on poorer urban areas, thus increasing the potential impact on African-Americans.

The widespread use of mobile phones and the wearing of body cameras means that there is more evidence about police violence and its impact that did not exist previously. This has not prevented the Right from smearing individuals such as George Floyd who died while in police custody in May 2020. Cases such as Floyd's are used by the Right to support deeply entrenched notions of black criminality and justify the police response. However, it is clear that the CJS and wider social policy discriminates in other ways, and that the overall impact of these forms of discrimination is the development of mass incarceration.

As noted earlier, Lloyd and Whitehead (2018) present mass incarceration as an inevitable outcome of neoliberal economic and social policies. Mass incarceration is a way of managing and disciplining urban, minority communities. Wilson (2011, 2012) outlined the devastating impact of deindustrialisation on the urban poor. The loss of relatively well-paid unionised jobs saw the development of the service economy; however, the replacement jobs in the service sector were often part-time and certainly did not carry with them healthcare and other benefits. To these huge challenges faced by poor urban communities was added the damage done by drugs and related crime. These issues disproportionately impacted on African-American communities.

There is what might be termed a 'standard narrative of mass incarceration', which is, perhaps, most closely associated with Alexander (2012). The broad thrust of this argument is that the 'war on drugs' in the 1970s and 1980s resulted in a huge rise in the prison population in the US, mainly driven by the incarceration of millions of people for low-level drugs offences. The 'war on drugs' was targeted at poor urban areas and this exacerbated the already massive racial disparities within the US criminal justice system. Alexander (2012) argued that these moves created a new caste system. It is not simply the over-representation of black males in the prison population that needs to be considered. Alexander (2012) outlines the way that a whole series of measures, such as felon disenfranchisement laws and housing laws, mean that formerly incarcerated persons are excluded from civic society. The new caste is predominately African-American. Alexander (2012) argues that these developments have to be seen in the context of the wider politics of race and the Civil Rights movement. Here, mass incarceration and its aftermath is understood as part of an attempt to undo the progress of the mid-1960s.

Elements of this standard narrative are challenged by the US legal scholar Pfaff (2017). It should be emphasised that Pfaff (2017) is arguing for prison reform and an end to mass incarceration. However, in challenging the traditional narrative of the expansion of the penal state, his work also calls for a different approach to ending it. There are two major areas where Pfaff (2017) departs from previous explanations. The first is the nature of offences that drove the development of mass incarceration to the turning point of 2010, when prison numbers began to fall. Pfaff (2017) argues that it is violent offences – rather than low-level drug offending – that are the main driver of the expansion of the prison population, though, in many instances, these offences may well be related to drugs. Here, Pfaff (2017) makes the hugely significant point that the response to concerns about rises in violent offending has been to call for longer and tougher sentences. To reduce the prison population effectively will require something of a shift in wider societal attitudes. Longer sentences for serious offences are often politically justified by the populist narrative that they not only punish individuals and protect potential future victims, but also demonstrate the strength of outrage and disgust at such offences. There is an implicit assumption here that a long period of imprisonment is what *all* victims of violent crime want to happen to the perpetrators (Simon, 2007). Such notions are based on an individualised analysis of the core drivers of violence that see such offenders as somehow cut off from wider society (Sered, 2019). This allows us to ignore the structural drivers of violence: inequality, racial discrimination, poverty, poor housing, poor education and the lack of community services (Wilkinson and Pickett, 2009). Sered (2019) argues that the core features of the penal state – racism, social shaming and the exposure to brutality – mirror the factors that result in people being incarcerated. Thus, the official policy responses to violence are based on the very features that create it. In looking at alternatives to long prison sentences as responses to violent crime, both Pfaff (2017) and Sered (2019) acknowledge that this will involve often difficult societal conversations about the nature and value of punishment.

The second area where Pfaff (2017) departs from the standard narrative is in his discussion of the role of the federal government. He argues that the focus on federal issues obscures the fact that prison systems at the local and state level lie at the root of mass incarceration. This therefore requires a deeper analysis of the specifically local factors that are responsible for the rises in the use of imprisonment. For example, in her examination of the closure of asylums in Pennsylvania, a state that had one of the largest mental health systems in the post-war US, Parsons (2018) shows that the failures of deinstitutionalisation, a fear-driven politics of mental illness and fiscal conservatism combined so that closing mental hospitals helped to feed the expansion of incarceration. The importance of the work of scholars such as Parsons is that it highlights that local factors played a role in the rise in incarceration rates and must therefore also play one in reducing them. Broader lessons can clearly be drawn. For example, Parsons's (2018) work emphasises that wider investment in mental health services must form part of the work that will end mass incarceration.

Pfaff (2017) places a focus on the role of prosecutors. He argues that prosecutors make hugely significant decisions about who is charged, the nature of the charges and plea bargains. He sees this group as being one of the key drivers of the increased use of imprisonment – often in the name of victims – but their role is little discussed and is largely out of the political spotlight. Pfaff (2017) argues that mass incarceration is an ineffective way to combat crime, particularly as there is limited support for those who are released from prison. The estimated US$80 billion that is spent on prisons and jails does not include the wider financial, social, emotional and physical costs that mass incarceration imposes on individuals, families and communities. The reframing of mass incarceration as an issue of human and civil rights, rather than one of law and order, means that these broader societal harms can be properly acknowledged.

The movement to end mass incarceration

Lloyd and Whitehead (2018) make a comparison between the triangular slave trade of the 1700s and contemporary mass incarceration. They identify the sides of the contemporary triangle as the 'neoliberal polity, the reproduction of social insecurity and the modernized transformation of criminal justice and penal policy in the direction of exclusionary punishment and prison' (Lloyd and Whitehead, 2018: 60). If we are to see parallels between slavery and mass incarceration, then one area to consider in more depth is how 'the peculiar institution' was abolished. What are the lessons that can be drawn? Hague (2007) presents a narrative of the abolition of the slave trade as one of the great achievements of British history. This approach plays to a traditional vision of Britain and the British Empire as a liberal progressive force that spread the alleged values of the Enlightenment across the globe. A figure like William Wilberforce is thus given a central, heroic role. There is not the space here to examine these issues in more depth; rather, it is raised because there may well be parallels between the forces that led to the abolition of slavery and modern movements to end mass incarceration.

Largely based in the US, there is now a growing movement that is calling for reform of the CJS and the end to mass incarceration. This movement includes organisations such as *Black Lives Matter*, think tanks such as the Vera Institute, the Stop Mass Incarceration Network and local community groups and academics. For example, the Vera Institute explicitly frames the issue as a civil rights one:

> America is at a tipping point. In a country that continues to lead the world in locking up its own people, mass incarceration has emerged in recent years as a defining civil rights issue. A movement has blossomed in which formerly incarcerated people lead alongside diverse and influential allies, powerfully capturing what's at stake: that runaway use of incarceration dehumanizes poor people and people of color, damages already marginalized communities, does not advance public safety, and siphons public resources with no social benefit. (Vera, nd: no pagination)

As in the Abolitionist movement, the media has been used very effectively to raise awareness and discussion of the issues: Alexander's (2012) *The New Jim Crow* received wide media coverage and became a driver for reform; Eugene Jarecki's (2012) documentary 'The house I live in' traces the impact of the 'war on drugs'; and the impact of the 'war on drugs' featured across David Simon's five-season TV epic *The Wire*. Although not a commercial success at the time, *The Wire* has subsequently been lauded as one of the greatest shows on US television. Set in Baltimore, it examines the wider social impacts of deindustrialisation, alongside the impact of the 'war on drugs' (Penfold Mounce et al, 2011). In presenting mass incarceration as an issue of civil rights, these campaigns make reference not only to the campaigns of the 1960s, but also to the era of slavery. Alexander (2012) explicitly makes this comparison. The comparison is made in the film the *13th*, though was made most publicly by John Legend and Common in their acceptance speech when they won an Oscar for 'Glory', their song in the film *Selma*. In his acceptance speech, Legend called for reform of the US criminal justice system, stating: 'There are more black men under correctional control today than there were under slavery in 1850'. This statement needs to be placed in some context as the US population is clearly significantly higher than it was in 1850. The 1850 Census found that approximately 90 per cent of the population of 3.6 million African-Americans were enslaved; today, one in 11 African-Americans are under some form of correctional supervision. Ada Du Vernay, the director of both *Selma* and the *13th*, then made the 2019 Emmy-nominated mini-series *When They See Us*. This series tells the true story of the wrongful conviction of five African-American and Hispanic teenagers for the rape of an investment banker who was jogging in Central Park. The series explores the ways that the prosecution and media use a series of long-standing racist tropes in the case, for example, comparing the boys to wild animals. President Trump, a prominent New York businessman at the time of the case, took out a series of newspaper adverts calling for them to be executed – even before they had been convicted. This series and other documentaries, such as *The Kalief Browder Story*, are playing a key role in bringing the brutality of the US penal system to wider attention.

Conclusion

The development of mass incarceration cannot be separated from other social and economic changes. The growth in inequality and the shredding of the welfare state (Giroux, 2011) are clearly drivers of the prison boom. These are features of neoliberalism. The attack on the social state has been a sustained one that has lasted for over 40 years but has been accelerated in the UK by the policy of austerity that was introduced by the Coalition government in 2010. Austerity's architects may have presented it as a response to a national emergency; however, its main aim of shrinking the role of the welfare state places it firmly in the libertarian tradition that flows from Hayek (2014) and Friedman

(2009). The demonisation of the poor as feckless and workshy shares key elements with Murray (1990); in fact, its roots can be traced back to Booth's representation of poverty in Victorian London (Cummins, 2018). Welshman (2013) demonstrates the way that problem families and communities have been rediscovered and redefined at fairly regular intervals ever since. In this tradition, poverty is not regarded as a structural issue; rather, its causes are the individual moral failings of the poor. As Lloyd and Whitehead (2018) show, the retrenchment of the welfare state has been accompanied by the expansion of the penal state. 'Workfare' and 'prisonfare' can thus be regarded as deeply interconnected. While recognising the centrality of race to these issues, the model that Lloyd and Whitehead present offers, at best, only a partial explanation for mass incarceration.

The current prison system is a site of the exploitation of labour, with prisoners being paid meagre wages to fight forest fires being a recent example (Lopez, 2018). Major corporations in the US and elsewhere are making profits from virtually all aspects of incarceration. The prison regime is increasingly brutal and violent, with a series of reports from individual prisons and Her Majesty's Inspectorate of Prisons (HMIP) highlighting appalling conditions in jails in England and Wales. Hall (2016) has highlighted the ways that not only major institutions, for example, banks and leading universities, but also citizens, made profits from the slave trade. There are echoes of this in the way that major corporations have invested in aspects of the penal state. Through shareholding and pension funds, individuals are also connected to the prison–industrial complex. The question here is whether this stands comparison to the role of chattel slavery in the development of modern capitalism. The economic impact of slavery and its key role in the foundation of modern capitalism (Williams, 2014) far outweighs the exploitation that occurs in the current prison system. The 'triangular trade' that was at the heart of the slave trade is a key element of Lloyd and Whitehead's comparison. The links between neoliberalism and modern penal policy are not as well defined and clear cut as those between the legs of the triangular trade. While in no way defending conditions in prison or the injustices of the current modern penal system in the UK and US, chattel slavery and all its horrors remain distinct. Mass incarceration and the racial discrimination inherent within it may be viewed as one of its legacies.

4

Exploring the Punitive Turn

Introduction

This chapter will explore the ways that the rise of the New Right in the mid-1970s and the subsequent dominance of neoliberal ideas had a profound influence on welfare and penal policy. One of the main themes in this volume is that these two areas are inextricably linked. This is not simply to say that they follow the same trajectory or that they can be used as the axis of a graph. Hinton (2016) shows that the development of US President Lyndon B. Johnson's Great Society programmes took place as the foundations of the modern US penal state were taking shape. The failure of these programmes to prevent the explosion of urban riots in the late 1960s was used by opponents of a broader social state to argue that *all* such programmes were futile and a waste of public money. The result was a consensus that saw increased use of imprisonment in the penal sphere and conditionality and surveillance in welfare as the solutions to the problems of poverty. A similar pattern emerged in the UK in the Blair years: the greater investment in social and welfare programmes did not prevent the continued rise of the penal state. This is partly because of a strategic decision by New Labour that it would not allow its opponents to portray it as weak on crime. It also reflects the communitarian values that underpinned the New Labour project. The analysis presented here is influenced by Simon's (2007) notion of *Governing Through Crime*, discussed in more depth later. Simon (2007) examined the politics of law and order in late modernity. Crime and punishment are clearly always political matters. The same is also true of welfare policy. However, until the election of right-wing governments in the late 1970s and early 1980s, there had been something of a consensus on law and order. Hall (1979) was the first to note that the Conservative

Party under Margaret Thatcher was breaking this mould. In doing so, as in other areas, Mrs Thatcher presented herself as being on the side of ordinary voters and against an elite – in this case, a liberal elite of penal scholars and policymakers in the CJS who focused on rehabilitation at the expense of punishment. This chapter will examine two key events in the period – the Strangeways Riot and the murder of Jamie Bulger – and discuss their wider impact on penal and social policy.

Crime and punishment

Crime and punishment raise huge ethical and philosophical issues. Before discussing the politics of law and order, I will explore this area from a range of perspectives. Crime and punishment is a key area of public policy. This is reflected in the fact that it has been explored from a range of perspectives and disciplines, including law, criminology, sociology, philosophy and psychiatry. Durkheim and Foucault, in producing a wider social theory, use the study of punishment as a sort of case study or starting point for their analysis. As Wright Mills (2000: 3) observed: 'neither the life of an individual nor the history of a society can be understood without understanding both'. This seems particularly relevant to the study of the CJS and the individuals who become wrapped up in it.

Foucault (2012) opens *Discipline and Punish* with the death warrant of Damiens, who had attempted to assassinate Louis XV and was executed in 1757. Damiens was subjected to a range of torture before his death. For Foucault, the level of brutality – not a term Foucault would necessarily use or approve of – inflicted on Damiens was not simply due to the nature of his crime; rather, it reflects the cultural attitudes and power dynamics of the period. All crime was regarded as a sort of assault on the bodily integrity of the king. Prisons and responses to crime do not exist in a vacuum, and we cannot divorce them from the wider political and cultural context. The CJS is part of the political, economic, social and moral order of any society. In analysing the shifts and turns that have brought us to the current position where imprisonment is such a deeply entrenched institution within late modernity, we have to examine all these factors alongside the history of the institution itself. Pashukanis (1978) argued that in capitalist society, punishment has to be viewed through the ideological conceptions of wider society. Punishment is thus a form of exchange: an offender pays their debt to society by serving a prison sentence. This focus on an economic influence appears to marginalise one of the most significant aspects of wider society's response to crime: the emotions that it generates, such as fear, anger, disgust and bewilderment. The cases discussed in this chapter are examples that generated huge waves of public emotion that had an influence on the development of penal policy.

Foucault (2012) saw the development of the prison as a way of analysing the dynamics and operation of power in modernity. For Foucault (2012), the technologies of disciplinary power that were and are used in the prison system are illustrative of how power functions. This is not to say that all systems are like prisons; rather, it highlights the continuities between the prison and wider disciplinary processes. Foucault (2012) shows that there has been a shift from the spectacle of the gallows to the bureaucratic and often hidden exercise of power. In the prison, disciplinary power operates in such a way as to produce useful 'docile bodies'. It does this by the manipulation of time, space and the body of prisoners. While the prison regime does this, we can identify other areas where similar techniques are used, for example, workplaces, schools and factories. This would include the creation of case records, systems of classification and the assessment of individuals by specialist professionals. One of the features of modernity that Foucault highlights is the increasing fracturing of professional claims to specialist knowledge. This is particularly apparent in the CJS, for example, Seddon (2007) outlines the way that female prisoners have been much more likely to be regarded as suffering from some form of psychological condition, which is the cause of their offending. For Foucault, Foucher's prison timetable, which detailed the daily activities of a Parisian prison, is not a form of progress; rather, it is simply a new technology of power and can only to be understood in the context of the cultural shifts that led to its creation and implementation.

There is a danger that this analysis of the atomic physics of power does not take full account of the fact that the exercise of power is inevitably met by some form of resistance. This occurs on an individual and a group level. Foucault (2012) argues that modernity had seen a shift in the role and aim of the processes of government. This shift means that governments have become much more focused on the condition of population rather than simply the exercise of sovereign power. 'Governmentality', as Foucault termed it, combines the notion of government and the exercise of rationality. This is possible because of the development of modern forms of the collection of information and statistical analysis, for example, in areas such as public health. Foucault (1982) emphasised the importance of active subjects, in the sense that modern citizens become heavily involved and increasingly responsible for the government of their own behaviour. This reaches its ultimate manifestation in modern neoliberalism (Brown, 2015,

2019). The cultural trope of individualism that has become so powerful means that all citizens are seen as having a much greater responsibility in areas such as health. There are some positives to this; however, there is something of a government double shuffle in evidence. By individualising problems, governments are able to ignore the social factors and determinants of health (Marmot, 2010; Karban, 2016), as well as the social and economic inequality that underpins them (Wilkinson and Pickett, 2009). This individualising approach also means that the solutions lie in individual behaviour rather than broader social welfare programmes.

Reading the graphic description of the execution of Damien and the contrast with Foucher's timetable, one might conclude that the severity of physical punishment has decreased in modern society. Physical punishments such as public flogging have disappeared from liberal democracies, though there are always calls for their return. The death penalty was effectively abolished in the UK in 1966. Despite attempts to reintroduce it, at the time of writing, it seems unlikely that its supporters will be successful. In the UK, the discourse of human rights has seen a focus on the conditions in prisons, though the media, particularly tabloid newspapers, has been promoting a discourse that prison conditions are 'too soft'.

Durkheim (2006) emphasised that punishment has huge symbolic value. It is not simply a series of physical acts; rather, it carries with it the moral condemnation of wider society. One can view public executions as the ultimate manifestation of this expressive function. Media and popular cultural representations of law and order now fulfil this function of creating a moral universe where criminals are seen as other. Durkheim saw punishment as creating and reinforcing social and community ties. In doing so, he moves the focus from the administrative apparatus of punishment to its wider social functions. His analysis is very much concerned with the emotive aspects of punishment: the symbolic denunciation that the process of arrest, prosecution and imprisonment entails. These processes are seen as a series of social rituals that contain and express the anger of the community at the violation of social bonds that crime entails. However, as Foucault and later scholars have emphasised, this focus on the role of punishment in the creation of social bonds overlooks the fact that these processes result in social division rather than social bonds. Once they have served their sentences, prisoners remain stigmatised and marginalised. Alexander (2012), in her analysis of race and the CJS, shows that the modern US system effectively excludes formerly incarcerated individuals from elements of modern citizenship. For example, 'convicted felon' legislation in a number states means that those who have served a sentence are not allowed to vote in any future elections.

Adler and Longhurst (2002) identify three discourses of imprisonment: rehabilitation, normalisation and control. They go on to examine three means that are linked to these discourses: bureaucracy, professionalism and legality. In a sense, these discourses are always present in debates about the development of penal policy. One way of exploring the development of mass incarceration is to suggest that the discourse of control has become dominant and excludes others, particularly rehabilitation, which seems to have almost disappeared from these debates. The discourse of control focuses on longer sentences and harsher prison conditions. It is an exclusionary discourse and plays to some of the key tenets that make up the basis for penal populism (Garland, 2001). The dominant concern of this narrative is the harms that violent and, particularly, sexual offenders have inflicted on individuals and wider society. These are, of course, vitally important issues; however, these offenders do not constitute a majority of offenders. At its core, this approach sees *all* offenders as having rejected the core values of society. In doing so, they have surrendered all future claims to liberty. Thus, society needs protection from this group and prison is the most effective way to ensure the safety of the majority of citizens. Colvin (1981, 1992) saw imprisonment as a function of the state specifically designed to control those populations who were regarded as surplus labour in capitalist societies. This traditional Marxist approach does not fully engage with the symbolic role of the major institutions of the CJS.

The 1970s saw a number of radical prisoners' groups formed across the world. In France, Foucault (Macey, 1993) was a key figure in the Group d'Information sur les Prisons (GIP), a prisoners' rights group founded in 1971. In 1971/72, there were over 30 riots in French prisons (Carrabine, 1998). In the US, there is a history of political radicalisation in prisons. For example, in his biography, Malcolm X (1965) outlines how he became a member of the Nation of Islam while in prison. Bauman (1989, 1991) identified two means of regulation in late-modern capitalist society. The first was the seduction of the consumer society. As well as the constant generation and regeneration of demand for consumer products, seduction involves, in fact, requires, the creation and recreation of an individual identity. Bauman suggested that those excluded from consumer society – the marginalised or 'failed consumers', as he termed them – are subject to repressive systems of government intervention.

The prison writings of George Jackson became key texts in the radical racial politics of the late 1960s and early 1970s. His murder took place before the Attica Prison Riot of 1971. Thompson (2017) outlines the way that the riot marked a political shift. For example, the Kerner Commission (1968) was established in the aftermath of the urban riots that took place across US cities in the 1960s, and its report was unequivocal: 'white society ... is deeply implicated in the ghetto. White institutions created it, white institutions maintain it, and white society condones it.' The Kerner Commission warned that the US was so divided that it was poised to fracture into two radically unequal societies – one black, one white. The government response should be a range of employment, education and welfare measures, combined with a commitment to tackling racism and structural disadvantage.

The naked and indiscriminate use of force ordered by Governor Nelson Rockfeller was partly driven by his political ambitions. However, Thompson (2017) shows how the brutal quashing of the Attica Prison Riot marked a huge shift in penal politics. In the aftermath of the carnage of the retaking of the prison, a powerful official narrative was developed. This narrative not only placed the responsibility for the deaths on the prisoners, but also painted them as brutal savages. It thus became a key factor in the wider disillusionment with attempts at liberal or rehabilitative approaches. The outcome of this was ultimately Martinson's (1975) 'nothing works' thesis, which suggested that programmes that were based in social investment to combat crime and rehabilitate offenders were doomed to fail and thus a waste of public funds. This argument was then taken up by the New Right in the 1980s, who appealed directly to middle-class and working-class voters, over the heads of the so-called 'penal policy establishment'.

Governing through crime

Simon (2007) argues that the period of mass incarceration is the culmination of a series of trends in penal and broader social policy. The result can be viewed as a new form of statecraft or governmentality – 'governing through crime'. Simon (2007) broadens the scope of his analysis from the process of legislating for and managing criminal behaviour, which is something that all states have undertaken. Simon (2007) examined what impact the perceived dangers of being a victim of crime has had on a range of behaviour and choices that citizens make. It is important that these responses are based on perceived dangers rather than some form of rational statistical analysis. Our responses to crime and the possibility of being a victim are often more likely to be based on emotions. Thus, we can see a number of cultural trends that are the result of a fear of violent crime. For Simon (2007), examples include the increase in sales of sports utility vehicles (SUVs) in the US and the rise of the gated community. Throughout areas of daily life, including schools and schooling, a fear of violent crime lies at the root of a number of policy developments. Simon (2007) was writing in the US context, where there are higher rates of violent crime. However, one can see that similar developments have occurred across other liberal democracies with lower crime rates, particularly of violent crime.

Governing through crime is a result of the economic and political crisis of the late 1970s and early 1980s. These economic and political difficulties led to questions about the effectiveness and legitimacy of government. Simon (2007) notes that law and order became politicised in a way that it had not been in the post-war period. In the social-democratic, Keynesian post-war evolution of penal policy, there was a general consensus among politicians, policymakers and academics. This consensus saw prisoners as individuals in need of welfare services that would rehabilitate them and enable them to play a positive role in society. The politicisation of the law-and-order question was a feature of the elections that returned neoliberal governments in the US and UK throughout the 1980s. Simon (2007) argues that the victim of crime, particularly violent crime, came to act as the dominant model of citizenship. He provides several examples where violent crime has had a direct impact on the election process. The most famous of these is the case of Willie Horton, a convicted murderer who raped a woman while he was on a period of weekend leave. This case was used by George Bush Sr in an attack advert on Dukakis in the 1988 presidential campaign. In 1993, a 12-year-old schoolgirl, Polly Klaas, was kidnapped and murdered by Richard Allen Davis. Following the public and political response to this appalling crime – Governor Wilson spoke at the funeral – Mike Reynolds, whose own daughter had been shot, used the case to support his campaign to introduce Proposition 184. This led directly to the introduction of the 'three-strikes' law in California, which has been such a driver of mass incarceration. As Simon argues, the logic of such policies is to replace the perceived weakness of liberal courts and judges with a clear populist response. In this process, the individual and ultimately social costs of mass incarceration are ignored. Simon (2007) outlines the ways in which the optimism of penologists in the 1970s that the prison as an institution might well disappear has been replaced by mass incarceration. Schrag (2004) outlines the 'neo-populist' terms in which law-and-order debates are consistently framed. As Garland (2004) suggests, this includes an element of distrust of experts, policymakers and political elites. The political Right has successfully exploited these populist themes.

Simon (2007) observes that all violent crime poses difficult political questions for governments of all persuasions. These problems were particularly acute for parties of the Left. Parties of the Right were able to portray them as 'weak on crime', 'on the side of the offender not the victim' or 'too concerned with the rights of criminals'. This was a hugely successful political strategy. However, it is based on the assumption that victims and offenders fall into two distinct, separate categories with no overlaps, as well as minimises or excludes the possibility of rehabilitation. The success of this strategy led to a significant shift by social-democratic parties in their positions on crime, offending and prison. The Blair New Labour governments are perhaps the best example of this shift, as illustrated by the fact that they did not halt the rise in prison numbers but, in fact, continued the policy of prison expansion. Garland (1996) notes that modern governments recognise that there are clear limitations as to how effectively they can deal with crime, while, at the same time, acknowledging that this is a hugely significant political issue. Therefore, increasingly punitive strategies are employed because they can be presented as evidence of the state's clear commitment to tackling the issues. Simon (2001, 2007) argues that the assumptions that underpinned much of modern penality ruptured as part of the crisis of legitimacy in the 1970s. This leads to a form of social and political nostalgia for older forms of penal policy and regulation, including boot camps and chain gangs in the US. These calls are based on an implicit assumption that these historic forms of regulation were successful.

The Strangeways Riot

Strangeways high-security prison opened in 1868. A classic of Victorian prison design, its iconic watchtower remains a distinctive feature of the Manchester skyline, a brooding brick presence at odds with the chrome and steel that now dominates. Strangeways is best known as the scene of the longest prison riot in British history. It unfolded as prisoners rebelled against the poor conditions at the prison and was supposed to have changed the face of the penal system forever. In 1980, the BBC showed a fly-on-the-wall documentary about the prison, which brought to wider attention the appalling conditions in the prison: there were no toilets in the cells, so prisoners had to use a bucket and 'slop out' every morning; prisoners had a shower and a change of clothes once a week; the prison was overcrowded; and prisoners were spending long periods, often 23 hours a day, 'banged up'. Not surprisingly, the documentary showed that there was a general air and tension within the prison. At the time of the riot in 1990, media reports of the background to the disturbances painted a picture of a prison regime that was very similar to the one outlined in the TV documentary over ten years earlier.

Three days before the riot, the Chief Inspector of Prisons had published a largely favourable report, outlining the progress that had been made at Strangeways since the Fresh Start initiative of 1987. This was swept aside by the events of early April 1990. The riot began at a service in the chapel on 1 April. The original disturbance rapidly spread and soon the prisoners had taken over the prison. The riot lasted for 25 days (for a detailed discussion of the timeline of the riot and its aftermath, see Carrabine, 1998). Soon after the takeover began, prisoners started to appear on the roof. A number remained throughout the protest, creating a sideshow for the press and Manchester commuters. One prisoner greeted the locals and the media with a cry of 'Good morning, Manchester'.

Within days, unrest had spread to 20 other prisons across the country. The tabloid press reported that prisoners were being murdered and told lurid tales of kangaroo courts being set up to try prisoners on remand for sex offences. They said 20 people had died at Strangeways. In the end, these claims turned out to be exaggerated; however, two people had died – a guard and a prisoner. It also became clear that vulnerable prisoners had been subjected to appalling violence. When the riot eventually ended, 23 of the prisoners were sentenced to a total of 140 years' imprisonment. The iconic jail had been destroyed and the rebuild would ultimately cost more than £100 million. The prison was renamed HMP Manchester after the riot but the Strangeways name has remained in common usage.

The Strangeways Riot was the biggest disturbance in British penal history. The discussion of the riot here is largely based on the Wolff Report (Wolff, 1991) of the inquiry into the riot and Carrabine's (1998) study of the riot and its aftermath. In many ways, it is perhaps surprising that there are not more disturbances within prisons. The most recent report of HM Chief Inspector of Prisons (2019) painted a portrait of a penal system lurching from one crisis to another. One of the most important things to bear in mind here is that individual prisons – even those that appear very similar from the outside – have very different organisational cultures, as shown by Liebling's (2000, 2002) work. This is the result of a number of factors, including the size of the prison, the mix of offenders and the management style of the governor and other leading figures. The official discourse is often that prison riots are caused by the influence of a relatively small group of the most difficult prisoners. These prisoners are often seen as those who have committed serious violent offences and lifers, who have less to lose if they confront prison authorities. As noted earlier, radical political figures are also regarded as the potential source of agitation. Thus, in official discourse, rioting confirms that those involved are beyond the pale or outside of accepted social norms. The act of riot is only a failure of the prison regime in the sense that the regime had not been severe enough.

Scraton et al (1991), in their analysis of the riot at Peterhead prison, take a very different approach. They argue that the riot was the inevitable outcome of the violent and repressive regime that was followed at Peterhead. There is an important point here about the use of power, which is clearly a very important issue in the prison context. However, the prison regime cannot simply be reduced to the exercise of force by the prison staff. Even in the most difficult of environments, there has to be some element of cooperation with the regime by prisoners; if not, it would be impossible to exercise power. The exercise of power raises questions of legitimacy. One of the ongoing complaints raised by prisoners at Strangeways was the use of an internal disciplinary system. Individual prisoners could be placed on report for breaches of prison discipline and there would then be a hearing before a governor who could sentence the prisoner, for example, to a loss of privileges. This system was clearly open to abuse as prisoners never felt that it was fair and legitimate. Carrabine (1998) provided detailed background to the build-up to the riot. As noted earlier, the prison had always had a poor reputation. It was seen as something of a 'dustbin' for the wider problems of the prison system, with troublesome prisoners from other parts of the estate being sent there. In addition, it was the reception prison from the Manchester courts, so there was a significant churn in the number of prisoners; it held prisoners on remand; and there were also prisoners from a wide range of backgrounds.

The governor at the time of the riot was Brendan O'Friel. In one of the ironies of these events, O'Friel was something of a reformer who recognised that changes needed to be made at the prison. Carrabine (1998) notes that the previous Governor, Norman Brown, was from a much more traditional background. The prison followed a much more military style of discipline and many of the officers were from military backgrounds. In addition, there was a very strong macho and drinking culture focused on the officers' mess. As Wolff (1991) notes, there was always an air of tension at the prison and rumours that there would be a major disturbance. It is, of course, difficult to know how seriously we should take these rumours. Carrabine (1998) emphasised that in the months leading up to the riot in April 1990, Strangeways had much in common with other prisons across the estate. The view of it as a human warehouse could have applied to other local prisons, for example, Walton Prison in Liverpool. Carrabine (2005) notes that terms such as 'mob violence' or 'riot' have been used by elites and official sources to discredit the grievances of those who take part in such disturbances. It is interesting to note that Wolff was very clear in locating the cause of the riot in what he saw as the legitimate concerns of the prisoners. This, of course, did not mean that he accepted the riot or the damage inflicted on the prison estate.

There is a danger of writing a history of the riot that sees it as inevitable. The conditions for the riot existed in many areas of the prison estate, including Strangeways on numerous previous occasions. Therefore, it is important to examine the contingencies. Useem and Kimball (1991) suggest that it is the disorganisation of the state rather than the organisation of the prisoners that is the key factor in the occurrence of a riot. It is clear from the Wolff Report (Wolff, 1991) that the prisoners were fairly astonished that the protest in the chapel escalated so quickly that they were soon in a position where they were in control of the prison.

In the aftermath of the riot, a public inquiry was established, headed by Lord Justice Harry Woolf, generally regarded as a liberal judge. When the inquiry reported its findings in 1991, it called for fundamental changes to be made to the prison system, including the abolition of the indefensible system of slopping out by 1996 and improvements to prison discipline, such as the establishment of a prison ombudsman to investigate prisoner grievances. Woolf also identified overcrowding as a key factor in the crisis in the prison system and called for smaller institutions. In 1993, Conservative Michael Howard became Home Secretary and there was a significant shift in the penal system. Howard was committed to the notion that 'prison works' and oversaw an expansion in the use of imprisonment. When the Strangeways Riot began, there were around 43,000 people in prison; now, there are more than double that number. The most recent report from the Chief Inspector of Prisons (HM Chief Inspector of Prisons, 2019) drew a bleak picture that had echoes of the system in 1990 prior to the Strangeways Riot. Suicides and bullying are still on the rise, and drugs are easily available. Shortages are putting staff at risk and the number of assaults has risen. One of the most important messages from the 1991report was the corrosive impact of overcrowding; it is simply not possible to manage a system in a humane fashion when prisons are so overcrowded.

The murder of James Bulger

In 1993, two ten-year-old boys were convicted of the abduction and murder of two-year-old James Bulger. The boys had abducted the toddler, who was out shopping with his mother, in Bootle on Merseyside. His mutilated body was found on a nearby railway line. The abduction and murder of children is a very rare event. That the perpetrators were themselves so young makes this case an even rarer crime. The two boys are the youngest convicted murderers in modern British history. Previously, in 1968, an 11-year-old schoolgirl, Mary Bell, was convicted of the murder of two young children in Newcastle. The Bulger case became the site of a whole series of debates. It was used as the basis for discussions about the causes of crime, the role of the media, modern parenting, the role of politicians in making decisions about sentencing and how the CJS should respond to children who commit the most serious offences. The CCTV image of Jamie Bulger being led away from the Strand Shopping Centre, holding hands with his killers, has become one of the most iconic images of the period. At the end of the trial, the judge decided that it was in the public interest that the names of the two boys should be revealed – Robert Thompson and Jon Venables. In the huge media coverage that followed, photographs taken of the two ten-year-olds when they had been arrested and charged were released. These photographs showed two small bewildered ten-year-old children. However, in the same way as the iconic photographs of Brady and Hindley (Cummins et al, 2019), for the tabloid press, these photographs were confirmation that the boys were cold, callous killers.

Legal issues

The Bulger case raised hugely important legal issues. These overlap with the broader social concerns that will be examined in more depth later. The age of criminal responsibility in England and Wales is ten years old, so children under ten are not charged with offences and do not appear in court. Until 1998, when it was abolished, the principle of *doli incapax* meant that those aged 10–14 could only be convicted if the prosecution could prove that they knew that what they were doing was 'seriously wrong'. This became, in effect, the crux of the trial of the two boys. In cases involving children, there are procedures in place that prevent the media disclosing the identities of defendants. The breaching of these procedures constitutes a very serious contempt of court. There is always a tension between the welfare and punishment streams of the CJS process. This tension is even more pronounced in cases involving children. The welfare approach argues that children who come into the most serious conflicts with the law do so because of underlying issues in their home and family life, and that it is these issues that need to be addressed to prevent further offending. Revealing the names of young offenders cannot assist in their rehabilitation. Throughout the trial, the boys were referred to as Boy A and Boy B. The opposing argument here is that the boys had committed such as serious crime that they should be treated as adults, which would involve the publication of their names. The fact that they had committed the most serious of offences was used as evidence to demonstrate the boys' maturity and sophistication.

Age is a somewhat arbitrary and often contradictory marker for legal participation in a range of significant social activities. The age of consent, when you can drive and when you can vote in the UK are all different. One of the features of the development of the penal state has been the way that juvenile offenders, particularly in the US, have become increasingly subject to adult sentencing processes. The boys were tried in an adult court in front of a judge and jury. There were some attempts to make the court more child-friendly, for example, the judge did not wear his wig and robes (Morrison, 1997). In 1999, the European Court of Human Rights (ECHR) found that the conduct of the trial, alongside the fact that the Home Secretary had set a tariff of 15 years that the boys should serve before being considered for parole, was a breach of the Human Rights Act 1998 (HRA). The conduct of the trial meant that it was impossible for the boys to participate fully or understand the process. Sereny (1995) saw the trial as a clash between two essentially mutually incomprehensible languages and discourses: on the one hand, the courts and legal system; and on the other, childhood and welfare.

The sentence for murder is life imprisonment. However, the trial judge sets a tariff – the length of time that the guilty person should serve. More recent reforms to sentencing mean that the judge can impose a whole life sentence, that is, the person will never be released. Justice Moreland emphasised that the backgrounds of both Boy A and Boy B were marked by hugely significant material, emotional and social deprivation. He recommended a tariff of eight years. This was increased to ten years by the Lord Chief Justice, Lord Taylor. The Home Secretary, Michael Howard, argued that the increased tariff was still inadequate. This was, in part, due to a campaign organised by *The Sun* newspaper. Howard argued that the shorter tariff would undermine public confidence in the CJS. In addition, Howard argued that the murder itself was an exceptionally cruel and sadistic one. The tariff was raised to 15 years. It was this process and the overtly political nature of the decision-making that the ECHR found was a breach of the HRA. In reviewing the case following the ECHR decision in 2000, the Lord Chief Justice reduced the tariff. When they were arrested and sentenced, the boys were placed in secure units, and the Lord Chief Justice argued that if they served a longer period, they would have to be transferred to a prison, which it was felt would bring with it the risk of revenge attacks. There were also concerns that a move from a welfare-oriented regime to a prison would undermine the progress that the boys had made. In 2001, David Blunkett, the then Home Secretary, concluded that the boys did pose a threat to the public and they were released on life licence. They were given new identities for their own protection. Venables has been imprisoned twice in 2013 and 2017 for offences related to the possession of child pornography; however, Thompson appears to have been successfully rehabilitated.

A moral panic

In outlining his model of a moral panic, Cohen (2002) highlighted the fact that they were often driven by concerns about crime and or the behaviour of young people. Hall et al (2013) emphasised that crime becomes the centre of wider unease, and noted that the panic is really about something other than the crime itself. This insight is particularly relevant here. Hall et al (2013) argue that crime in general and the particular crime that instigates the moral panic are viewed as a symbol or index of the disintegration of the social order. The broader social, economic and political context provides the backdrop for the rise of the moral panic. In this case, the early 1990s was a period of economic recession and increasing unemployment. The Major government that had narrowly and surprisingly won a victory in the 1992 general election was under immense political pressure following the UK's exit from the Exchange Rate Mechanism in September 1992. In a number of other areas, it was seen as a weak and vacillating administration.

During the course of a moral panic, the focus will shift to a particular aspect of the crime or behaviour. For example, in this case, there was huge media coverage of the horror film *Child's Play 3*, in which a doll comes to life and murders a child. It was suggested that one or both of the boys had watched the film several times (Morrison, 1997). The Bulger case received huge media coverage around the world. In the UK, the case became the focus of a wider concern about youth crime.

In the swirling media commentary, the facts of the case, particularly its rarity and the age of the perpetrators, were lost. The two ten-year-old perpetrators came to stand for all young offenders and there followed a series of tough law-and-order policies.

It is likely that all parents and carers have experienced that moment of icy horror when they lose sight of their child in a shopping centre, on a crowded beach or at a tourist attraction. This is a scene that has become a staple feature of crime and domestic drama. The overwhelming majority of these cases are quickly and happily resolved. This case came to crystallise a series of modern fears about the risks that children are seen to face. Even though the perpetrators were children, the abduction and murder were part of wider concerns about predatory paedophiles. Crimes against children raise particularly strong emotions, and cases of abduction are often viewed as symbolising the end of a notion of community (Cummins et al, 2019). Hay (1995) contrasts the coverage in the Bulger case with that given to the murder of 70-year-old Edna Phillips. Mrs Phillips was murdered by two teenagers, Maria Rossi and Christina Molloy, in Wales in July 1992. They were given indefinite life sentences in 1993. The judge at the trial described the perpetrators as products of a 'lawless modernity'. Christie's (1986) notion of the perfect victim is important here. There is regrettably something of a hierarchy of victims which means that crimes involving, for example, children are much more likely to get wide media coverage. The creation of the idealised victim trope excludes or marginalises those who are somehow seen as being culpable in some way. A glaring example of this is the treatment of the murders of sex workers by the media and often law enforcement agencies (Wattis, 2017, 2019).

Hay (1995) notes that younger children like Boy A and Boy B were more likely to appear in the media as idealised innocent victims of crime. In this case, they were presented as the embodiment of evil. However, the case became a jump-off point for much wider concerns about youth crime. Hay (1995) highlights the confusion that society faced in trying to switch from seeing such young children as potential victims to the notion that they had committed such an abhorrent act. In this confusion, it seemed that Boy A and Boy B were representative of a lost generation of feral children, rudderless and amoral. This led to some rather wild jeremiahs about the state of modern Britain. An editorial in the *Sunday Times* in November 1993 is an example of this. Written after the trial, the editorial claimed that the case meant that parents and wider society will look at children in a completely different way following the details of the case and the outcome. It concluded that 'Parents everywhere are asking themselves and their friends if the Mark of the Beast might not also be imprinted on their offspring' (Sunday Times, 1993). The contrast between this rhetoric – it is surely unlikely that parents were engaged in such conversations and moral turmoil – and the comments from the trial judgment about the material and emotional deprivation that were features of the boys' upbringing could not be starker.

The media, particularly *The Sun's* campaign about the length of the sentence, had an unusually direct influence on decisions made in the case. The unusual nature of this case and the huge public interest and media coverage meant that it was inevitable that there would be wider comment from leading politicians. Three days after James Bulger's body was found, Prime Minister John Major gave an interview to the *Mail on Sunday*. The *Mail* newspapers are strongly pro-Tory and supporters of what they see as traditional family and social values. This includes a very authoritarian stance on law-and-order issues. Major, perhaps not too surprisingly, had struggled to establish his own image – Mrs Thatcher cast a long shadow. Major was often ridiculed as being not only grey and dull, but a weak and vacillating figure in comparison to the Iron Lady. In this interview, he tried to establish his credibility as being strong on law and order, stating that 'Society needs to condemn a little more and understand a little less' (Macintyre, 1993) – this is an excellent example of penal populism, that is, a call to 'ordinary people' over the heads of academics and policy officials. The statement encapsulates the idea that the CJS has become too concerned with the rights of offenders and ignores victims. Within the quote, there is also an implicit call for a return to traditional approaches to discipline and so on – the quote is dripping in nostalgia.

Major was struggling to hold the parliamentary Conservative Party together over divisions about the UK's role in Europe. At the Conservative Party conference in 1993, where Michael Howard made his famous 'prison works' speech, Major announced a 'Back to Basics' initiative, which was a call for a return to traditional family values. In that year, Tory ministers had made speeches attacking single mothers, portraying them as benefit cheats and so on.

The 'Back to Basics' speech was an attempt to bring the Conservative Party together around a core set of principles and policies. It is noteworthy that the way that crime was seen is a key issue. Taylor (2004) argues that we understand, debate and analyse complex social and political issues via metaphor. The metaphor of crime as a cancer is a recurring one, carrying with it as it does the notion of the corruption of the body politic by an external and hostile agent. To extend the metaphor, it also carries with it the need for radical surgery and treatment in order for healing to take place. The Back to Basics initiative fell apart in a series of stories and scandals about the private lives of Tory MPs.

The shadow Home Secretary at the time of the murder of James Bulger was Tony Blair. At that point, Blair was a rising star of New Labour and, along with Gordon Brown, one of the leading figures in the party. Blair was determined that New Labour would not be outmanoeuvred on issues of law and order by his opposite number, Michael Howard. As noted earlier, penal policy had been seen as one of the policy areas where, in the Thatcher years, the Labour Party had been seen to lose contact with its traditional working-class base. Blair was influenced by the Left Realist criminology that had emerged from critical criminology. Writers such as Young (1991, 1992) argued that there was a need to recognise and acknowledge the impact that crime had on working-class communities. At the same time, the Left needed to develop credible alternative penal policies and not abandon the field to the populist Right. This approach chimed with Blair's communitarianism and rights-cum-responsibilities agenda. As he makes clear in his biography, Blair's response was to make the case a symbol of a 'Tory Britain, in which ... the bonds of social and community well-being had been loosened, dangerously so' (Blair, 2010). In an earlier speech, Blair had described the case as a 'hammer blow against the sleeping conscience of the country' (Cohen, 2002). In the post-Thatcher period, there was a greater politicisation of the issues of law and order. The result of this was that the centre ground shifted rightward. The expansion of imprisonment and other punitive approaches did not end under New Labour; in fact, they became more deeply entrenched.

The prison population increase

The prison population in England and Wales nearly doubled over the period 1993–2012, despite the generally falling crime rates and a period of sustained economic growth. The expansion of the use of imprisonment that had been given such impetus under the political stewardship of Michael Howard continued under his New Labour successors. There were 41,800 people in prison in June 1993; by June 2012, that number had risen to 86,000. This increase was mostly due to rises in two groups: those sentenced immediately to custody; and those recalled to prison for breaking the conditions of their release. After

1993, the courts were sentencing more offenders to prison for longer periods. One of the impacts of penal populism is that the long-term consequences of decisions taken by politicians are often felt long after they have left office or faded from public memory. Over the period 1945–92, the average increase in the prison population was 2.5 per cent per year. In the period before the Strangeways Riot, the prison population had actually fallen slightly; however, over the period 1993–2008, the prison population grew by an average of 4 per cent per year.

The increase in the use of custody was driven by a range of factors. Tougher sentencing meant that the proportion of adult offenders receiving an immediate custodial sentence rose from 16 per cent in 1993 to 27 per cent in 2011. Alongside this, offenders were sentenced to longer periods in prison. The Criminal Justice Act (CJA) 2003 introduced Indeterminate Sentences for Public Protection (IPPs). When the sentence was abolished, it was replaced with a 'two-strikes' policy which meant that an offender convicted of a second serious sexual or violent offence could be sentenced to life imprisonment. Offenders serving sentences for serious violent or sexual offences would only become eligible for parole when they had served two thirds rather than half of their sentence.

Young offenders post-Bulger

Penal policy in the second half of the period that this volume covers is dominated by the introduction of legislation that had the overall impact of sending more people to custody for longer periods. The arrival of Michael Howard at the Home Office can be seen as the start of these trends but they have continued ever since. No home secretary since Howard could really be described as liberal, let alone progressive. Simon (2010a) argues that we have become addicted to the use of imprisonment, despite its manifest failings in doing what it claims to do. An exhaustive list of the relevant legislation in this period is not provided here; rather, alongside the IPP, the examples are illustrative of the trends in penal policy. The 1993 CJA amended the 1991 Act so that previous convictions could once again be taken into account. The result was that more offenders were sent to immediate custody by the courts. The Crime (Sentences) Act 1997 introduced a mandatory three-year minimum sentence for a third domestic burglary. Its provisions also included a mandatory minimum seven-year sentence for a third class A drug-trafficking offence. As well as introducing IPPs, the CJA lengthened periods on licence, which meant that recalls were more likely. Suspended sentences were also extended again, increasing the number of breaches. The CJA also established that sentences imposed for breaches had to be longer than the order breached. The 2008 Tackling Knives Action Plan meant that there was an expectation that courts would impose tougher sentences for the possession of knives and offensive weapons. In 2010, new guidelines introduced a new tariff of 25 years, increased from 15, for a murder committed with a knife or other weapon taken to the scene.

Conclusion

This chapter has argued that the responses to the Strangeways Riot and the Bulger case can be seen as watershed moments in the politics of law and order. The increased expansion of the penal state has its roots in this period. Morgan (2014) notes that recorded crime had been rising in the 1970s and 1980s. There was a further period of increased recorded crime, driven by the explosion in the use of heroin, which peaked in 1992. There were 2.5 million recorded crimes in 1979 compared with 4.5 million in 1990, an increase of 80 per cent (Morgan, 2014). The home secretaries in the early Thatcher governments, for example, Willie Whitelaw and Douglas Hurd, were very much from the One Nation wing of the Conservative Party but this did not prevent the introduction of measures such as the 'short sharp shock'. Hurd was committed to prison and wider penal reform, and oversaw the introduction of the 1991 CJA. The White Paper that led to the introduction of the CJA argued that prison 'was an expensive way of making bad people worse' (Home Office, 1990). Newburn (2003) sees the 1991 CJA as an attempt to establish community punishments as genuine and robust, and in which wider society could have confidence. As noted earlier, the Major government faced a crisis in legitimacy very soon after he became Prime Minister. The appointment of Michael Howard from the right of the party, with a combative reputation and a commitment to overturning what he saw of the dominance of a liberal penal policy agenda, was a move to re-establish political legitimacy and control. Home secretaries will always have a key role in penal policy. Howard became a key figure in challenging the Home Office approach (Newburn and Jones, 2007). Howard himself has said that whenever he proposed the greater use of imprisonment, Home Office officials argued that it would not work, while Treasury officials baulked at the increased spending that such moves would involve. Whatever barriers he faced, Howard was able to overcome them. In his time as Home Secretary (1993–97), the prison population rose by 40 per cent. When his former parliamentary shadow, Blair, was elected in 1997, he was not going to allow New Labour to lose its hard-won reputation on law and order. The home secretaries of the Blair era, Straw, Blunkett, Clarke and Reid, could never be described as progressives. The result was that there was a significant shift rightwards in penal policy and the prison population continued to grow.

5

The Third Way in Welfare and Penal Policy

Introduction

This chapter will explore the rise of New Labour, focusing on its approach to welfare and penal policies. New Labour marked a departure from more traditional social democratic policies that previous Labour administrations had adopted. In response to Thatcherism, New Labour tacked to the right, concerned that it would be seen as weak on crime. The prison population continued to grow in this period. In addition, New Labour introduced a new approach to welfare policies. These echoed the 'tough love' approach of the Clinton Democrats, introducing new forms of conditionality to the welfare system.

The birth of New Labour

There are many echoes of the early 1980s in post-Brexit politics. The Conservative Party has shifted further to the right and there is little doubt that Mrs Thatcher is the political heroine of current cabinet ministers, such as Priti Patel and Dominic Raab. In fact, they were co-authors of a Thatcherite polemic *Britannia Unchained* (Kwarteng et al, 2012), which was a programme to complete the Thatcherite revolution. As well as attacks on British workers, it included a proposal for the privatisation of the National Health Service (NHS). In the 1983 general election, the Labour Party under Michael Foot presented a radical programme. It included the nationalisation of the top 200 FTSE-listed companies, leaving the European Union (EU) and a commitment to nuclear disarmament. It was famously described by Labour MP Gerard Kaufman as the 'longest suicide note in history'.

The 1983 general election was a disaster for the Labour Party. Mrs Thatcher was returned with an overall majority of 144; Labour lost 51 seats. The election was its worst performance since 1918. In the rout, three future leaders, Tony Blair, Gordon Brown and Jeremy Corbyn, were returned as MPs for the first time. The roots of New Labour are in the defeat of 1983. Michael Foot resigned and Neil Kinnock was elected leader. Kinnock was from the left of the party but led it from the centre, and a process of 'modernisation' began. This included the expulsion of Militant (a Trotskyist grouping within the party), the abandonment of support for unilateral nuclear disarmament and the party becoming pro-EU. From the post-Brexit referendum perspective, it is interesting to note that its opposition to the EU was used by its opponents to argue that Labour was 'not fit to govern'.

As well as moving the party to the centre, Kinnock made it a slicker operation. Despite this, he lost two general elections in 1987 and 1992. After his resignation, John Smith was elected leader. Smith was from the centre of the party and the strong Labour tradition. Smith had been a junior minister in the previous Labour government and was regarded as a fierce opponent, highly intellectual and an outstanding parliamentary performer. Smith faced a very changed political landscape. The Thatcher revolution had seen a profound ideological shift, while Labour was still, to a certain extent, hamstrung by its statism of the 1970s. Of course, its opponents portrayed it as old-fashioned and committed to a return to the 1970s. However, it would be naive not to recognise that attitudes to the role of the socio-economic changes that followed the oil crisis of the early 1970s had a profound influence. Manufacturing industries – mining, steel production and shipbuilding – had declined to the point where they barely existed in comparison to their prime. This meant that union membership – the bedrock of Labour support – had subsequently declined. The rise of finance and service sectors, and with it the casualisation of employment (more part-time and short-term contract work), made it more difficult for unions to recruit and organise members. There was also a significant shift in the role of women in the workforce. These factors combined to produce huge changes in the political and economic life of the country and the number of trade union members dropped significantly.

Smith launched a 'prawn cocktail offensive' to woo potential supporters in the City and convince them that Labour would not completely reverse the changes that had taken place under Thatcherism. He also established a Commission for Social Justice headed by Sir Gordon Borrie (1994). The commission was committed to a vision of social equality and identified key principles of social justice, as follows:

- the equal worth of all citizens;
- the equal right to be able to meet their basic needs;
- the need to spread opportunities and life chances as widely as possible;
- the requirement that we reduce and, where possible, eliminate unjustified inequalities. (The Commission on Social Justice, 1994)

The final report included a recommendation from Tony Blair on the cover, describing it as 'essential reading for everyone who wants a new way forward for our country'.

Smith died of a heart attack in 1994 and was succeeded by Tony Blair. The principles that the Social Justice Commission outlined are classic social-democratic ones. However, the impact of the Thatcherite shift meant that they appeared more radical. Blair's creation of New Labour was an attempt to create a new political approach that married a dynamic laissez-faire economy with greater investment in public services.

Just as the assessment of David Cameron's political career will ultimately focus on the Brexit referendum, it is inevitable that the decision to go to war in Iraq will be the defining event of the Blair years. The rightwards political shift and electoral successes of Thatcher and Reagan in the 1980s saw nominally progressive parties across the world tack to the right. This was true of the Clinton and Blair administrations, as well as of the Hawke and Keating administrations in Australia. Influenced by Fukuyama's (1992) 'end of history' argument, Blair concluded that the old politics of the Right and the Left was dead. It should be noted that in this model, fairly crude notions of political poles are used. The Right is presented as embodying the Hayekian free market and the Left as committed to a somewhat exaggerated level of state intervention. Blair essentially accepted the basic premises of market-oriented approaches and sought to marry these with a new model of the state. Blair had successfully constructed a new progressive coalition of urban elites and more traditional Labour voters by skilfully appealing to the social liberal while also adopting recognisably social-democratic policies, with a focus on investment in public services. This was given intellectual gloss and termed the 'Third Way' by Giddens (1998), not free market capitalism and not 1970s' statism.

In 1997, New Labour faced an environment where there had been significant underinvestment in public services – in particular, the NHS – for some time, with a third of the UK population living in poverty. The new government sought to move towards a new attitude and approach to poverty and inequality, and coined the term 'social exclusion'. This was a classic New Labour combination of structural and individual factors, including unemployment, low income, poor housing, high-crime environments, family breakdown and poor skills. As a term, 'social exclusion' was positive in that it captured the overall impact of the increase in inequality that had occurred over the previous 18 years of Tory government. However, it is also a term that depoliticised notions of inequality. The Blairite mantra was that equality of opportunity rather than equality of outcome should be the concern of progressive governments. This period saw greater investment in public services and social programmes such as Sure Start that were aimed at tackling childhood inequalities.

The Third Way and Blair's general political philosophy were heavily influenced by the communitarianism of Etzioni (1993). For all his modernising progressive rhetoric, Blair's political programme was based on very traditional notions. Communitarianism (Etzioni, 1993) focuses on key social institutions, such as the family, schools and voluntary groups, as sites for the development of values. It is wary of state institutions and organisations, which are regarded as remote and bureaucratic. There is an acceptance that society has a wider duty to support citizens but concerns about the creation of dependency and the failure to challenge anti-social behaviour. These themes are not that far removed from the criticisms of the welfare state that can be found on the Right. Blair's moves in these areas are often presented as a cynical election move to attract Tory voters but they are seen here more as an accurate reflection of his underlying beliefs. In an important move, Blair shifted from a traditional social-democratic concern with equality to a more nebulous focus on equality of opportunity. Communitarianism has within it the roots of the more punitive approaches to social policy that characterised much of the later New Labour project (Butler and Drakeford, 2001).

New Labour also argued that globalisation and the power of huge corporations such as Apple meant that the power of governments was diminished. The role of government was to create an environment where a dynamic economy would provide the basis for investment in public services.

The state and the Third Way

Despite the sometimes visceral anti-statism that is a feature of market fundamentalism, the demands of late-modern capitalism generate a key role for the state (Chang, 2010). One example that illustrates this is that the free market has never been able to ensure that the whole population receives an education; to achieve this, the state has had to intervene. Globalisation and deindustrialisation have created a two-track economy, with one track being precarity (Standing, 2011) and the other requiring an increasingly well-educated workforce. Blair was very keen on soundbites, one of which was 'education, education, education'. Blair saw education, developing skills and increasing the number of graduates as one of the keys to modernising the British economy. It was also argued that expanding higher education would be an engine of social mobility. Savage (2015) outlines the complexity and enduring nature of the UK's class system and the way that educational achievement is one of the key determinants of individual position within these structures.

One of the key aims of both the Thatcher and Major governments was to introduce the private sector into public services. This was partly motivated by a desire to reduce the size of the state but was also based on the idea that the private sector was dynamic, innovative and efficient in comparison to the bureaucratic and rule-bound public sector. Skelcher (2000) used the term the 'hollowing out' of the state to describe the processes that led to the establishment of a range of independent agencies to take on state functions. Pollitt and Bouckaert (2004) outline this development of 'new public management' (NPM). NPM was an attempt to introduce some elements of the market, including a form of competition, to public services. In this model, it was important that there was a purchaser–provider split to break up perceived monopolies. The result was the creation of regulation and inspection regimes for public bodies. The most high-profile of these was probably the Office for Standards in Education (Ofsted) for schools and eventually children's services. Alongside this, the public were given more information about the performance of public institutions: there were league tables for schools and hospitals; organisations were given targets, for example, waiting times in accident and emergency departments; and patients, pupils and parents suddenly became customers. NPM led to the development of an audit culture and the bureaucratic structures to service it. Public sector professionals felt undermined and were soon drowning in a sea of audits and inspections. These trends were particularly apparent in the areas of welfare and penal policy, and while they began under the Tories, they were not reversed under New Labour.

New Labour and penal policy

'Tough on crime, tough on the causes of crime' became one of the most famous phrases of the Blair era. Blair had risen to prominence as shadow Home Secretary. His opposite number was Michael Howard, later to become leader of the Conservative Party. In many ways, crime and penal policy is a defining issue of New Labour's domestic agenda. Crime, and the allegedly weak official response to it, was one of the elements in Thatcher's construction of the 'nation in crisis' narrative. It should be noted that this narrative conflated a series of issues, including immigration, welfare, trade unionism and progressive education. Simon (2007) has highlighted the way that law and order became increasingly politicised and polarised. Blair (2010) was determined that he would not be outflanked on these issues. His response to the murder of James Bulger focused on such issues as parenting, which had much in keeping with Tory responses and those in the tabloid press. Blair (2010) openly acknowledged that he was determined that he would not be seen as weak on this issue as there was a clear perception that crime and penal policy was a vote-loser for Labour in the 1980s. The party was seen as 'being on the side of the offender' and too concerned with nebulous human rights issues. From this perspective, there is a clear offender–victim binary division and human rights in the CJS become a zero-sum game. All these factors combined to make law and order a signature New Labour issue. Alongside these political realities, it should be acknowledged that the strong streak of communitarianism in New Labour's and Blair's political thought meant that they took a different perspective to crime than predecessors.

Blair's ideas in this field were partly influenced by Young's (1991, 1992, 1999) Left Realism perspective. The influence of Left Realism can be seen in the Crime and Disorder Act 1998 (CDA). Left Realists argued that prison should be used as a last resort and in cases where there was a danger to the community. The CDA introduced measures that ensured offenders had to take responsibility for their actions. Alongside this, there were policies to tackle social and economic exclusion. Young (1991, 1992) argues that previous law-and-order policies had focused on a triangular relationship of offender–victim–state. However, this missed an important part of the jigsaw: the wider community. Young later felt that New Labour policy had become too influenced by the underclass discourse.

Anti-social behaviour

If there is one term in this field that is most closely associated with New Labour, it is 'anti-social behaviour' and the policy response: the Anti Social Behaviour Order (ASBO), with the term 'ASBO' entering modern slang. Anti-social behaviour has clearly always existed. Influenced by Left Realism, New Labour argued that it was the poorest communities that suffered most from the impacts of anti-social behaviour: neighbourhood nuisance, graffiti, complaints about noise and litter, and so on. There is a long-standing recognition within criminology that the most deprived, particularly urban areas, experience high crime rates, alongside higher levels of anti-social behaviour. Alongside these factors, they are also areas were residents have greater levels of dissatisfaction with the police (Finney, 2004; Thorpe and Wood, 2004). Anti-social behaviour was seen as having a cumulative impact on the community and was also regarded as an issue that liberal elites often downplayed or ignored. The policy was part of an attempt to reconnect with voters on issues that directly affected their lives. In addition, anti-social behaviour was seen as the first step to involvement in more serious criminal activity. These were the sorts of repeated incidents that either took up a great deal of police time or, conversely, would lead to complaints that the police were ignoring local concerns. Anti-social behaviour was also seen as preventing the regeneration of communities as it would deter new investment.

ASBOs were introduced by the CDA, though an ASBO is a civil matter. They can be issued where there is 'conduct which caused or was likely to cause harm, harassment, alarm or distress' (CDA, 1998). Examples of such conduct include begging, intimidation, vandalism and shoplifting. The idea behind the ASBO was that there are a range of cases that are difficult to prosecute in the criminal court but have a hugely disruptive impact on the lives of neighbours and the wider community. The problems in developing criminal prosecutions included supporting witnesses to come forward. For an ASBO to be issued, there was a two-stage test for the court to consider:

- the defendant had committed acts causing or likely to cause harassment, alarm or distress;
- an order was necessary to protect persons from further anti-social behaviour.

Even though an ASBO was a civil matter, a breach could lead to a sentence of imprisonment. There were concerns that ASBOs were, in effect, criminalising social policy and that they were used too frequently or inappropriately (NACRO, 2002, 2006). It was also felt that the ASBO became something of a badge of honour among some young people. However, the most fundamental criticism was that the ASBO did not deal with the underlying causes of the behaviour.

Home Office guidance initially indicated that ASBOs should not be used in cases involving those under 18. This was later amended so that 12–17 year olds could be made subject to them. In the case of someone aged under 16 who had breached their conditions, they were not imprisoned; rather, a parenting order was issued. In the first two-and-a-half years of their existence, 58 per cent of ASBOs were given to a person under age 18; in another16 per cent of these cases, the person was aged 18 to 21 (Campbell, 2002). In itself, this is perhaps not that surprising: younger people are much more likely to be involved in such behaviour because of their immaturity and so on. The concern with these figures is that the individuals were putting themselves at risk of custody if they breached the order, which was also more likely because of their age.

Tony Blair gave his first major speech as Prime Minister on the Aylesbury Estate in South London. This was a highly significant choice of venue as the estate was seen to exhibit all the problems associated with so–called 'sink estates' and anti–social behaviour. After the introduction of the ASBO, tackling anti-social behaviour became a central plank of New Labour policy (Home Office, 2003). It was clear that this was an ideological as well as a political commitment. Blair made clear that the ground that New Labour had made in this area was not to be surrendered lightly. In addition, it was linked to New Labour's wider position as Blair argued that with rights come responsibilities. This is one of the most significant shifts of the Blair regime. He spoke of a new consensus on 'law and order' but while Blair might have wished to claim the credit for this shift, it was a combination of factors. The 'broken windows' perspective (Wilson and Kelling, 1982) had not only focused on the importance of what had been seen as low–level criminal behaviour, but also called for a stronger official response to it, claiming that this would lead to reductions in more serious crimes. Alongside this, the focus on anti-social behaviour was part of the underclass discourse that had become more influential across all political discourse. In his speech on the Aylesbury Estate and subsequently, Blair accepted the main propositions of the underclass discourse. The response was to support communities and residents to assert community norms. Flint (2019) outlines the key role that conditions for social housing tenancies had in these processes.

Blair's (2010) new consensus on law and order was very much a rejection of 1960s' liberalism, which he saw as at the heart of that decade. This is something of a cliché but it is one that has deep appeal – the notion of a golden age. Blair argued that what was required was a form of tough love, that is, a reassertion of social order and a refusal to accept anti-social behaviour or any excuses put forward to explain it. Blair's communitarianism meant that he did not accept the Thatcherite mantra that there is no such thing as society. However, membership of New Labour's society was dependent on the acceptance of a stronger social contract (Levitas, 1996, 1998). These moves meant that the CJS was given a new, more explicitly ideological role on the side of the victim and the law-abiding majority (Squires, 2006). Despite this, Blair's critics on the Right still attempted to portray New Labour as being on the side of offenders. The HRA became hugely symbolic here as it was seen as the ultimate evidence that a culture of rights was open to exploitation and abuse by undeserving criminals. On the Left, New Labour was seen as pandering to Tory prejudices for electoral gain.

As well as the rhetorical shift, penal policy in the New Labour era was marked by the introduction of new forms of managerialism in the CJS. This included new forms of organisational structures and the involvement of the private sector. Alongside these, there were new techniques and uses of technology, with the CDA introducing the electronic tagging of offenders. Scott (2007) argues that in the New Labour period, the two most important policy documents were *The Halliday Report: Making Punishments Work* (Halliday, 2001a) and the 2003 CJA, which was based on it. Halliday (2001a) sought to cement popular support for the CJS by introducing what Scott (2007) terms a 'form of punitive rehabilitation' that would bring together community punishment and prisons. These policies were based on an assumption that prisons, if properly resourced and managed, could perform a key rehabilitative role. From the New Labour perspective, prisons had been unable to fulfil this role under the Tories because of chronic mismanagement and overcrowding. As Scott (2007) notes, in this model, prison is somewhat miraculously transformed from punishment to an opportunity. Scott (2007) terms this 'making punishment work'. This leads to the introduction of a range of offender management programmes that are based on cognitive-behavioural approaches. The efficacy of these programmes, such as a sex offender programme, has subsequently been called into question (Guardian, 2017). These programmes completely ignore any structural factors in offending.

The National Offender Management Service (NOMS) was created in June 2004. One of the aims of this reorganisation was to encourage greater private sector involvement in both prisons and community-based rehabilitation, with one effect of creating these new structures being the outsourcing of services. This means that governments are no longer responsible or able to be held effectively accountable for failing institutions. If a prison is privatised and is deemed to be failing, then a new more effective and efficient contractor can be brought in (Clarke and Newman, 1997). For New Labour, the shift in focus towards victims meant that the aim of sentencing was to ensure that the public is protected.

The period 1979–2015, which is the focus of this volume, saw a significant increase in the prison population. As noted in Chapter 4, the upward trend in prison numbers was given a significant boost by Michael Howard's period as Home Secretary. In December 1992, there were 40,600 prisoners in the prisons of England and Wales, the lowest recorded rate in recent times; however, in May 1997, the prison population had grown to just over 60,000. This trend was not reversed by the arrival of New Labour; by June 2007, it was over 81,000. As ever, the failings of the prison as an institution led to calls for more and more prisons, with tougher regimes (Scott, 2007). New Labour was not to be moved from the path of penal expansionism; in fact, it could be said to have revelled in its new tough law-and-order image. At the Labour Party conference, Jack Straw stated that they had achieved their aim of making Labour the party of law and order.

The Stephen Lawrence Inquiry

Stephen Lawrence was an 18-year-old black British student who was murdered in a racist attack in London in April 1993. He was waiting at bus stop with his friend, Duwayne Brooks, when they were attacked. Stephen was stabbed after being chased by a gang of five youths. The investigation into the murder was marred by a mixture of racist stereotyping and incompetence. The initial police investigation appeared to assume that this was a gang-related murder, despite evidence from witnesses at the bus stop that it was a racially motivated attack. Members of the local community also provided the names of suspects and indicated that they had been involved in other violent racist attacks in the area. It was later revealed that the officer in charge of the case did not know that it was possible to arrest a suspect on the grounds of reasonable suspicion. In April 1994, frustrated with the failings in the official handling of the case, the Lawrence family initiated a private prosecution against a group of five young men. The charges against two were dropped before the trial; the three remaining suspects were acquitted when the trial judge ruled that the identification evidence of Duwayne Brooks was unreliable. In February 1997, an inquest returned a verdict of 'unlawful killing'. The suspects had refused to answer any questions on the basis of advice given by their lawyers. The next day, the *Daily Mail* published a front page with a picture of the five suspects and the headline 'murderers', and challenged the gang to sue.

The Lawrence case came to represent long-standing issues within the black community and its relationship with the police. New Labour had included a commitment to hold a public inquiry in its 1997 manifesto. The inquiry was completed in February 1999 and its findings were published in the Macpherson Report (Macpherson, 1999), which proved to be one of the most significant and influential documents of the New Labour era. The report made a total of 70 recommendations. It accepted that racism had been a factor in the failure of the police to investigate the case properly and convict the perpetrators as there was clearly enough evidence to convict the members of the gang if the case had been conducted properly (Cathcart, 2012). The recommendations included measures designed to transform the attitude of the police towards race relations, as well as to ensure that the civil service, NHS, judiciary and other public bodies addressed racism. These recommendations were based on the definition of 'institutional racism' that the inquiry defined as follows:

> The collective failure of an organisation to provide an appropriate and professional service to people because of their colour, culture, or ethnic origin. It can be seen or detected in processes, attitudes and behaviour which amount to discrimination through unwitting prejudice, ignorance, thoughtlessness and racist stereotyping which disadvantage minority ethnic people. (Macpherson, 1999)

The recommendations included targets for the recruitment, retention and promotion of black and Asian officers. In addition, the report led to the creation of the Independent Police Complaints Commission. The inquiry also resulted in the abolition of the 'double jeopardy rule', which stated that people could not be tried for the same crime twice. Its abolition meant that if new and compelling evidence was discovered, then another trial could take place. In 2012, two of the original suspects were convicted of the murder.

New Labour and welfare

Despite wider investment in public services, welfare policy under New Labour did not mark a rupture from the Thatcher period. This can be seen in the continued 'modernisation' of the welfare state and the creation of new agencies. On the broader ideological front, Blair's 'anglicised communitarianism' (Deacon, 2000) had much in common with the Clinton administration, which had introduced a series of reforms to 'end welfare as we know it' in 1996. These shifts were part of moves of what Giddens (1998) termed the 'social investment state'. This term was used to mark a break with the traditional welfare state. New Labour argued that traditional welfare systems papered over the cracks by paying cash benefits to alleviate poverty. It was suggested that the benefit system thus created passive recipients of welfare and that a new dynamic system was required, which would provide 'investment in human capital wherever possible, rather than a direct provision of economic maintenance' (Giddens, 1998: 117).

The Chancellor of the Exchequer, Gordon Brown (1999), argued that tackling child poverty was a policy that would tackle other social problems, such as crime, drug misuse and poor educational attainment. This was not simply a matter of a social good; such investment would also have an impact on the economy and help to produce a more highly skilled, flexible workforce. The other side of the 'social investment state' was that a series of reforms would place conditions on claimants. The process of conditionality would be extended under austerity (Dwyer et al, 2019) but these policies were building on what went before.

In a series of speeches after he became leader of the opposition, Blair set out the New Labour vision. These speeches contained a number of key words that soon became clichés, for example, 'reform' and 'modernisation' appear frequently and were used almost interchangeably.

One of the noticeable influences of US policy developments was in the use of language, for example, 'social security' was replaced by 'welfare'. At first glance, this might appear a rather insignificant change. However, Garrett (2017) charts the way that the use of language and terms was a key part of the Right's war of position against the welfare state. By dropping the term 'state', welfare came to be used in its stigmatising sense that can be traced back to the work of Murray (1990) and Mead (1992). In the 1997 Labour manifesto (The Labour Party, 1997), proposals to reform the welfare state were a key component. In presenting these policies, Blair emphasised what he saw as their distinctive radical nature. Welfare reform would not be tied to the dogmas and failures of the old Left and the Conservative Right (Powell, 1999). Blair appointed Frank Field as minister for welfare reform with a brief to 'think the unthinkable'. Before he became an MP, Field had been Director of the Child Poverty Action Group and the Low Pay Unit. Field wanted to move away from the state provision of benefits to a Continental-style social insurance approach. However, this proposal never gained that much support and Field returned to the back benches.

In 1999, Blair wrote an article about the Welfare Reform Bill in the *Daily Mail* and stated that it would mean the 'end of the something for nothing welfare state' (Lister, 1998). Lister (1998) argues that the early New Labour period saw a move towards 'redistribution of opportunities': education, training and employment. In this change in focus, work and the market were seen as the solution to the problems of poverty. The aim of wider welfare policy should be to support communities and families so that children and young people develop the skills that they need for the modern job market. Miliband (1994) argued in terms that were largely indistinguishable from his Tory predecessors that the most powerful social policy was a dynamic economy. This approach led to the introduction of the minimum wage and the introduction of the Working Families Tax Credit scheme in 1999. These and other policies were all aimed at 'making work pay'.

New Labour's New Deal

The New Deal was the centrepiece of the New Labour welfare reform. It was essentially a workfare programme targeted at 18–25 year olds and was funded by a windfall tax of £5 billion on privatised utility companies. The aim of the New Deal was to reduce unemployment among young people. The New Deal created the power to withdraw benefits from those who 'refused reasonable employment'. The policy can be traced back to reforms in 1986, which had introduced compulsory 'Restart' interviews for those who had been unemployed for six months. Blair emphasised that these changes represented a new balance of rights and responsibilities. Claimants would face greater restrictions and would have to produce more evidence of the steps that they were taking to find employment.

Under the New Deal, claimants were called for an initial compulsory 'consultation session'. This session focused on improving job search and interview skills. In another typical New Labour feature, the training was provided by a third sector or private organisation, such as A4E. If this search was unsuccessful, to continue on Job Seeker's Allowance (JSA), they would have to follow one of the following four options:

• a subsidised job placement
• full-time education and training
• work in the voluntary sector
• work with the Environmental Task Force

Refusal to take part in one of these options led to sanctions and the withdrawal of JSA.

One of the consistent feature of attacks on the welfare state has been the targeting and scapegoating of single or lone parents – the terminology has changed over the time. In the Tory period influenced by the underclass discourse, lone parents, the overwhelming majority of whom are women, were portrayed as feckless, promiscuous and so on. They were viewed as exploiting an overgenerous welfare system and living in relative luxury on benefits. This reached its nadir in 1992. John Major had appointed an arch Thatcherite, Peter Lilley, as Secretary of State for Social Security. He made a speech to the Conservative Party conference that year in which he promised to 'close down the something for nothing society'. The speech was a pastiche of the Lord High Executioner's 'little list' song from *The Mikado* by Gilbert and Sullivan:

> I've got a little list | Of benefit offenders who I'll soon be rooting out | And who never would be missed | They never would be missed. | There's those who make up bogus claims | In half a dozen names | And councillors who draw the dole | To run left-wing campaigns | They never would be missed | They never would be missed. | There's young ladies who get pregnant just to jump the housing queue | And dads who won't support the kids | of ladies they have ... kissed | And I haven't even mentioned all those sponging socialists | I've got them on my list | And there's none of them be missed | There's none of them be missed. (Lawson, 1994)

Blair's government did not produce anything like this level of vilification directed at single parents. However, the New Deal for Lone Parents introduced in 1997 did signal a shift. The scheme was initially a pilot in which claimants with school-age children were to be invited into their local job centre and offered help and advice on jobs, training and childcare. Each individual would have a personal caseworker who would develop an individual plan of action for the claimant and allow them access to the services provided by the Employment Service. At the time, there were about 1 million lone parents claiming benefit and about half had children of school age. The programme started for 40,000 lone parents in eight parts of the country from July 1997 and became a national programme in October 1998. In an example of the carrot-and-stick approach, the government made changes to Family Credit, Housing Benefit and Council Tax Benefit to encourage lone parents to return to work. These were coupled with the Sure Start schemes and a national childcare strategy intended to improve the availability and quality of nursery provision.

Conclusion

Tony Blair was elected as an MP at Labour's then lowest point. From 1983, the party underwent a long and often painful transformation. When he left Downing Street in 2007, he had led Labour to three general election victories. Just as with Thatcher, when he left office, the country was very different to when he arrived. He had also produced a significant change in his main opponents. Cameron was more like Blair than both would probably be prepared to admit. In terms of social policy and style, there was a clear overlap between the two. They also both adopted an informal but essentially patrician style of government. The 2016 Chilcott inquiry into the Iraq War was highly critical of Blair's 'sofa' style of government, whereby he sidelined members of the cabinet when making major decisions. He shared with Cameron an obsession with being regarded as modern and a different kind of politician. In the areas of welfare and penal policy, Blair made major organisational changes and reforms but the underlying ethos could be seen as a mixture of traditional themes given a modern twist by the use of jarring buzzwords imported from the world of MBA-holders. The increased investment of the New Labour years came a cost.

The 1997 general election was a huge personal triumph for Blair. In 1979, Stuart Hall had written 'The great moving right show' (Hall, 1979), which not only was a trenchant analysis of the new political structure, but also posed a number of questions for the Left and how it would respond. After the success of New Labour in 1997, Hall wrote what can now be viewed as a companion essay, 'The great moving nowhere show'). Hall notes that Blair is evidence of the success of the Thatcherite project: 'Its aim was to transform the political landscape, irrevocably: to make us think in and speak its language as if there were no other' (Hall, 1998: 11).

Blair was at ease and fluent in the language of the market, and wary of using the language of the old Left. 'Equality' and 'redistribution' were replaced by 'equality of opportunity' and 'modernising'. The Third Way was really a hybrid joining together two previously clashing approaches. The left-wing element of the Third Way was based on traditional views that saw the institutions of the welfare state as a necessary buffer against the market. The right-wing element of the Third Way was a belief in the market and acceptance that it would produce inequalities. These would be worth accepting as the dynamism of the market would produce the necessary funds for investment in a revitalised and reformed public sector. This new public sector would be modelled on the enterprise and risk-taking of the private sector. Blair was at ease – far too at ease his critics on the Left would say – with the involvement of the private sector in health and other areas. Blair was convinced that the private–public sector debates were outmoded: users of public services – or consumers as they became – were not interested in whether the service was run by the public, private or third sector. Blair (2010) argued that it was the quality of the service that was important.

The Third Way was a curiously depoliticised form of politics – a 'politics without enemies' (Hall, 1998). This masked the reality. In welfare and penal policies, New Labour offered increased investment but with a more punitive response to those who did not take up the advantages of the social investment state. Blair is an excellent example of Fraser's (2016, 2017b) notion of progressive neoliberalism. He spoke the language of social movements fluently and he was committed to an inclusive rights-based politics. The language of progressive social justice has been colonised by the Right (Boltanski and Chiapello, 2005; Fraser, 2009), with increased conditionality in the welfare system becoming a way of creating opportunities.

Hall (1998) saw New Labour as a hybrid, that is, a social-democratic variant of neoliberalism. It viewed the market as the most powerful mechanism to move people out of poverty. Consequently, markets need to be as lightly regulated as possible if they are to function effectively and the modernisation of government requires the involvement of leading figures from business. This was a trend that Cameron followed with equally disastrous results. For example, in 2010, Cameron appointed Sir Phillip Green, the owner of the Acardia Group, as his efficiency tsar to oversee government spending. New Labour retreated from the party's historic commitment to the universality of social provision and created a social-democratic model of a 'market state'. This led to outsourcing and other features of the audit culture and NPM.

6

New Labour, New Realism?

Introduction

This chapter will explore three developments within the CJS system that occurred from the 1990s onwards under Conservative and New Labour administrations: Imprisonment for Public Protection (IPP), joint enterprise and the whole-life tariff. The chapter begins with a discussion of the influence of left realism on New Labour and how NPM led to significant changes across the CJS, and ends with a discussion of the reform of the Mental Health Act (MHA) and the notion of Dangerous Severe Personality Disorder (DSPD).

Left Realism

In this section, I will discuss the broad impact of the influence of Left Realism on New Labour's penal policies. Before he became leader and created New Labour, Tony Blair engineered a significant shifted in the party's position on law and order. He was determined that Labour would not be out manoeuvred by the Tories on penal policy. However, it would be a mistake to see this as purely a strategic political move as these shifts were underpinned by Blair's communitarian beliefs. These moves were a response to the Thatcherite law-and-order agenda and an attempt to reconnect with voters on this core issue. Left Realism emerged within criminology a decade before the election of New Labour. However, it is possible to see its impact on some key notions of New Labour policy. Left Realists were ultimately critical of the way that New Labour approached questions of community and crime.

Left Realism was most closely associated with the work of such criminologists as Young and Lea. It can be understood as a response to and a recognition of the political success of Thatcherism and penal populism. Hall was one of the first to identify the implications of the shifting political and economic trends of the 1970s. In 'The great moving right show', Hall (1979) saw that the mixture of economic liberalism and social conservatism that Mrs Thatcher represented was a new and influential political force. The article was published in January 1979 before Thatcher's election in May of that year. The post-war social-democratic settlement was unravelling at that point, most clearly in the Winter of Discontent (López, 2014). Hall's article was very prescient in that it recognised that 'Thatcherism' (a term that he coined) had a popular appeal. He then went on to outline the building blocks of its popular appeal. Thatcherism was able to position itself as representative of the 'ordinary' British citizen against the vested interests of the social-democratic welfare state, for example, radical trade unions and teachers. Social workers were also regarded as one of the groups using their position to impose progressive ideas and undermine traditional family values. Hall recognised these moves as an attempt by the New Right to demonstrate that it was on the side of those who worked hard, paid taxes and so on. These processes also entail the othering of groups such as the poor, welfare claimants and offenders. These processes were racialised, as *Policing the Crisis* (Hall et al, 2013) showed. Thatcherism combined some traditional Tory values with a commitment to radical solutions to the social, economic and political issues that had produced the crisis of the mid-1970s.

Policing the Crisis (Hall et al, 2013) is a classic study of the way in which moral panics reflect wider social and political disquiet. Hall et al (2013) sought to explore how and why particular themes, including crime and other deviant acts, produce such a reaction. They argue that social and moral issues are much more likely to be the source of these panics. There are certain areas, for example, youth culture, drugs or lone parents, where there are recurring panics. Hall suggests that the panic is triggered by an event and describes the ways in which these events cause 'public disquiet'. The response to this panic includes not only societal control mechanisms, such as the courts, but also the media, which becomes an important mediating agency between the state and the formation of public opinion.

One potentially fruitful approach to the analysis of Left Realism is to regard it as a reaction to the popular and electoral successes of Thatcherism. Penal policy became more, not less, Thatcherite under the leadership of John Major, particularly when Michael Howard was Home Secretary. Left Realism argued that progressive politics needed to engage with the realities of crime. The most important factor here is that working-class people are more likely to be victims of crime and that the impact of crime is most keenly felt in working-class neighbourhoods. Matthews (2010) argues that Left Realism sought to produce an account and response to crime that recognised the genuine harms that individual criminal acts could inflict on victims while, at the same time, not diminishing the harms caused by the crimes of the state and corporations. Right Realism and Thatcherite rhetoric focused on the impact of crime on victims. This was a powerful and popular message that excluded any account of the crimes of the elite or broader notions of social harm. In the Right Realist model, crime is simply a matter of individual morality. It does not examine the social conditions that underpin crime trends (Hall and Wilson, 2014).

Lea (1987, 1992, 2002) argued that in focusing on the crimes of the powerful and the injustices of the CJS, radical criminologists had marginalised the impact of crimes such as burglary, theft and domestic violence, which were often intra-class. Critical criminology's naive notions of offenders as class warriors and the general absence of policy suggestions had allowed the populist ideas of the New Right to dominate. Lea (1987, 1992; Lea and Young, 1993) sought to develop a critical analysis of the problem of crime that would lead to progressive policies. Lea (2016) argued that Left Realism developed as a reaction to the poles of Conservative law-and-order policies and what he terms 'Left Idealism', the term he uses for the work of Hall et al (2013) and others such as Gilroy (1982, 2013). Both these perspectives failed to engage with the reality of the impact of crime and policing. The result was that working-class communities suffered from both high crime rates and ineffective and racist policing. This was in addition to other deprivations and the damage that Thatcherite economic policies had inflicted. He suggests that the Left Idealism of Hall et al (2013) saw concerns about crime as being the result of a media-induced moral panic and naively portrayed working-class crime as a form of political rebellion. Left Realism sought to focus on the impact of crime on working-class communities.

Lea (1987, 1992) outlined what he termed the 'square of crime', with the four corners being: victims, offenders, the public and state agencies. The aim of Left Realism was to improve the relations between these four groups. For example, it was argued that improved relations between the police and communities would not only address the injustices caused by institutionalised racism and homophobia, but also lead to safer communities. Better relations would lead to improved confidence in state agencies and this confidence would then enable state agencies to carry out their roles more effectively. These processes would also avoid an increased focus on securitisation. Alongside these developments, greater social investment would tackle the underlying causes of crime.

Jeffery (2011) outlines a cynical narrative of late modernity and degeneration, where notions of community are swept aside to be replaced by forms of market fundamentalism and dystopianism. It is possible to view Left Realism, with its focus on the relationship between state agencies, communities and individuals, as an attempt to counter this. Lea (2016) argued that Left Realism was a call for a renewal of democratic accountability. There has been a fall in the sorts of street crimes that were of particular concern at the time of the development of Left Realism. However, there has been an increase in new forms of criminality – cybercrime, online sexual exploitation, fraud and money laundering – that have driven new forms of securitisation. Lea and Young (1993) saw the problems of law and order as part of broader questions of democracy and political accountability as democratic participation has an educative and integrative function. There was a focus on local crime and victimisation in Left Realist approaches. Effective policing is dependent on a flow of information from individuals and communities to the police. This is the case not just for individual crimes, but for much broader concerns. By making the police more democratically accountable to the community, it was argued that they would be regarded as legitimate.

The key figures of Left Realism were critical of New Labour's penal policy. New Labour governments included a series of home secretaries, such as Jack Straw, David Blunkett and John Reid, who could not be considered as progressive or 'soft on crime'. The prison population continued to rise and New Labour also introduced legislation and policy in response to terrorism that was attacked for its impact on civil liberties. For example, the 2003 CJA doubled the period of detention of a terrorist suspect for questioning to 14 days and the Prevention of Terrorism Act 2005 introduced the control order – later replaced by Terrorism Prevention and Investigation Measures (TPIMs) – which allowed for the effective house arrest of terrorist suspects. The Terrorism Act 2006, which was drafted following the 7/7 London Bombings in 2005, increased the period of detention of a terrorist suspect for questioning to 28 days. The initial proposal to extend this to 90 days was defeated in a House of Commons vote. It also included a definition of the offence of 'glorifying' terrorism.

Left Realism was criticised for having softened or abandoned a radical critique of capitalism and the CJS (Akers and Sellars, 2008). Matthews (2014) argued that Left Realism should be seen as a left-wing social-democratic project that was aimed at providing a counter-narrative to the dominant liberal-conservative consensus. Young (1999) was critical of New Labour's communitarianism, arguing that this led to a focus on marginalisation rather than reintegration. Policies such as ASBOs and the expansion of the use of imprisonment ultimately exclude. Young (1999) argued that the version of police accountability that was introduced became an alliance with 'respectable citizens', and community safety was based on exclusion (Lea, 2010). This was not the vision of increased police accountability and democratic oversight and community integration that was a key aspect of Left Realist perspectives.

New public management, policing and the criminal justice system

One of the features of the New Labour period was the continuation and extension of NPM across welfare and other services. NPM seeks to bring the wider principles of the market to public services. These reforms involve a shift in language and focus – users become customers, community and other groups become stakeholders, and so on. New Labour in office continued processes that had begun under the Major government. For New Labour, the price of investment in public services was reform.

At the heart of this approach is a fundamental shift in the nature of policing. Community policing, rather than being a reactive model, requires the police to work with local communities and relevant health and social welfare agencies to gain an insight into local problems (Skogan, 2008). Not all such problems are necessarily crime, but they will involve a police response. Such an approach acknowledges that the police cannot 'solve' the problem of crime on their own. It is also an implicit recognition that policing is often more concerned with the welfare of vulnerable people than the detection and arrest of offenders. The moves to a partnership approach began in the 1980s. Holdaway (1986) outlines that such local partnerships were met with scepticism, with the police regarding them as 'talking shops'. There has been huge progress in overcoming the clash of organisational cultures that created barriers to partnership working. At the heart of these was the command-and-control nature of the police compared to the more diffuse approach of welfare organisations (O'Neill and McCarthy, 2014). The 1998 CDA made involvement in such partnerships a statutory duty for the agencies. This was followed by the development of local neighbourhood policing from 2008 onwards.

The organisational changes and development of partnership working occurred at the same time as profound changes in social and other attitudes in the areas of race, gender and sexuality. Loftus (2009) examines what she terms the 'politicisation of diversity'. This term reflects the response of the police to providing an appropriate and adequate service to citizens from sexual, racial or other minority groups. The Macpherson Report (Macpherson, 1999) outlined historical failings and abuse in the policing of black and minority ethnic (BME) communities. Burke's (1994) research demonstrated that the discrimination and homophobia that gay and lesbian police officers faced reflected the response that these groups faced from the police. A Her Majesty's Inspectorate of Constabulary (HMIC) (1999) report concluded that forces were failing to provide an adequate service to gay and lesbian citizens. Loftus (2010) sought to revisit the notion of police culture – as outlined in the classic formulation. She identified that there was a tension between the changes in the policy landscape and the persistence of some of the police's cultural characteristics; in particular, the sense of 'them and us' was a persistent trope. This took two forms: the rank and file saw themselves as apart or often at odds with the senior management, as well as with the general public. The sort of openly racist comments that Holdaway (1983) reported in his classic study of policing were not present. However, Loftus noted that derogatory comments aimed at young working-class or marginalised communities were still present.

The sense of loyalty and being a member of the 'police family' was still present. This work, along with Brough et al (2016), noted the continued endurance of a strongly masculine aspect to police culture, despite the changes to recruitment and other initiatives. However, important shifts were identified. The first was the reduction in social rituals, particularly those linked to drinking. This was partly the result of social attitudes but Loftus (2010) also identified that the 'job' was no longer seen as the key aspect of officers' lives. Like other public services, policing was dominated by a culture of risk and risk management. McLaughlin (2007) argues that the aim of the diversity reform agenda has been to remove the worst aspects of Reiner's cop culture and create a modern organisational work culture. This is not simply a matter of organisations complying with legislation; rather, it involves a recognition of the benefits that diversity can bring, for example, by recruiting from a broader base, you bring new qualities to an organisation and the police can serve communities more effectively. The developments in this area overlap with the arrival of a new organisational structure that sees new forms of partnership working. O'Neill et al (2007) argue that police culture should be seen as simply the 'way things are done round here'. This underestimates the ongoing strengths of some of the traits of police work. The nature of the work is a key factor in its organisational and work culture. Loftus (2010) concluded that despite these changes, aspects of 'cop culture' clearly remain. This is because the fundamentals of policing remain, that is, engaging with often powerless or vulnerable people in difficult, tense and demanding situations.

One of the key features of NPM has been the development of what is termed the 'audit culture'. Shore and Wright (2015) summarise audit culture as the spread and application of the principles of financial accounting to measure the performance of individuals and organisations. It is one of the most significant features of modern organisations in both the private and public sectors. Audit processes have completely reshaped transparency and good governance, producing changes in the way that individuals and organisations function. This culture has led to the adoption of a series of key performance indicators (KPIs) for organisations such as schools, hospitals, police forces and prisons. Along with these targets, there has been the creation of a range of inspection bodies, such as Ofsted. The most trenchant criticisms of this approach are that it undermines professional autonomy and distorts the work of the organisation. It is argued that it is inevitable that in an audit, target-obsessed culture, senior staff will ensure that the focus is on meeting KPIs. KPIs are often very crude measures of the work of an organisation and are open to potential manipulation. Finally, audit culture is seen as diverting resources from the 'real' work of the organisation to meeting the demands of inspection. The weight of bureaucracy is seen as preventing professionals from getting on with their jobs. The CJS was far from immune from these developments in the New Labour period and this has continued under subsequent administrations.

Dangerous Severe Personality Disorder

In this section, I will briefly outline the development of the terms 'personality disorder' and 'psychopathology' before going on to examine the background to the Fallon Inquiry at Ashworth Special Hospital. This question of how the CJS and mental health systems should respond to those who have committed the most serious violent crimes or are felt to pose a risk to the public has always been a controversial one. The Fallon Inquiry was one of a number of inquiries into the special hospital system, and like many others, it called for its abolition. The policy response was to introduce a new category of individual with 'dangerous severe personality disorder', a category that was essentially an administrative, not a clinical, one. Arguing that these reforms played into a particular popular narrative about dangerous individuals is not to deny the potential risks involved here or to diminish the nature of the crimes committed.

Before examining the background to and the outcomes of the Fallon Inquiry (Fallon et al, 1999), it is important to consider the development of the controversial terms 'psychopath' and 'psychopathology', which were first coined by the German clinician Koch. At the heart of these debates are fundamental questions about the nature of personality, mental illness and treatment. These terms do not always refer to those who have committed crimes, for example, in *Snakes in Suits*, Babiak et al (2006) offered guidance on how to identify psychopathic traits in your work colleagues and how to survive working with them. In popular culture, the figure of the serial killer has become a modern urban monster. The wider societal relationship with them encapsulates or crystallises the modern fear of crime (Simon, 2007; Cummins et al, 2019). Grover and Soothill (1999) noted that the 'serial-killing industry' was booming, and the boom has continued in the 20 years since that paper was written and appears to show no signs of slowing down. The popular demand for films, dramas and 'true crime' accounts of these crimes appears to be insatiable.

Seddon (2007) noted that the issue of how the penal system and wider society should respond to offenders who are deemed mentally ill has been a recurring question of modernity. In 1904, the Royal Commission on the Care and Control of the Feeble-minded was established. One of its main concerns was to look at the position of those who were thought of as being 'mentally disordered' but were not being certified under the existing Lunacy Acts. The commission was concerned that a number of people who were considered 'socially dangerous' people were certified as medical opinion held that insanity could not be diagnosed on conduct alone. The commission proposed a new category of patient: the 'moral imbecile'. The 'moral imbecile' was regarded as mentally ill but also demonstrated 'strong vicious or criminal propensities on which punishment had little or no deterrent effect' (Royal College of Physicians, 1908). This concept was incorporated into the Mental Deficiency Act 1913.

In 1957, the Percy Commission examined the mental health law. The commission argued that the existing legislation did not adequately address the position of how to deal with offenders of higher intelligence who were thus not covered by the 1913 Act. The solution was the creation of a new legal category: the 'psychopathic patient'. The Percy Commission suggested that this group would include any type of aggressive or inadequate personality, which is a very broad category. The Percy Commission led to the Mental 1959 MHA, which defined 'psychopathic disorder' as a 'disorder or disability of mind, which results in abnormally aggressive or seriously irresponsible conduct'.

A 1959 Working Group on Special Hospitals concluded that psychopathic patients should be treated in separate units from mentally ill patients (Cummins, 2016a). The Butler Committee (1975) set out to review the treatment of 'mentally abnormal offenders'. It argued that the term 'psychopathic disorder' should be abandoned in favour of 'personality disorder'. The Butler Committee also recommended that a new form of indeterminate reviewable sentence should be introduced. Reed (1992), in *Review of Health and Social Services for Mentally Disordered Offenders and Others Requiring Similar Services*, recommended the creation of an extra 1,500 medium-secure beds in smaller units than the special hospital system. This review concluded that there was little research evidence of the effectiveness of various forms of treatment proposed for personality disorder. The legal, medical and philosophical issues that this creates were underlined by Coid (1992). In his research based on interviews at Broadmoor Special Hospital, he found that only 23 per cent of male patients and 31 per cent of female patients detained in the legal category of psychopathic disorder met the diagnostic criteria. Thus there was a clash between the legal and medical uses of the term. One might add that further confusion is created by the popular usage of the term 'personality disorder', which can take many forms, including borderline, narcissistic, anti-social, compulsive and histrionic (Coid, 1992). A diagnosis of personality disorder does not exclude mental illnesses.

In addition to the problems of diagnosis and treatment, one has to consider what the links are between personality disorder and offending. There is a danger of circular reasoning here: a person commits an offence because they are suffering a personality disorder and the evidence for the personality disorder is that they have committed an offence. The relationship between personality disorder and violence or offending behaviour is much more complex and diffuse. Professor Blackburn, in his evidence to the Fallon Inquiry, suggested that a personality disorder may contribute to the development of a deviant lifestyle that results in some form of offending.

The Fallon Inquiry

The MHA gives the courts powers to sentence offenders to be detained on conviction. In such circumstances, the most common disposal is a section 37 (MHA) Hospital Order. These powers are contained in Part III of the Act. The most important differences between this and civil detention are clearly that the offender will have committed an offence and approved social workers do not have powers; it is a matter for the magistrates or judges. The courts make these decisions on the basis of the medical evidence put before them. In theory, a hospital order can be the sentence of the court in any case where there is not a mandatory sentence. It could not therefore be used in murder cases as there is only one sentence: life imprisonment. The Crown Court has powers under section 41 to issue a 'restriction order'. The net effect of a restriction order is that the patient cannot be discharged without the permission of the Home Secretary or a mental health review tribunal headed by a judge. Such patients are known as section 37/41 patients and if they are successful at appeal, they can be given an absolute or conditional discharge.

The Fallon Inquiry was established to examine events on Lawrence Ward, Ashworth Special Hospital. The ward had been a specialist unit for patients suffering from personality disorders. There are three special hospitals in England: Ashworth (which is the amalgamation of two older hospitals, Moss Side and Park Lane), Rampton and Broadmoor. These institutions are an uneasy mix of hospital and prison. In theory, the individuals are patients and therefore receiving treatment. However, all the patients are deemed to pose a very serious risk to the public. It is possible to be admitted to a special hospital without having committed any offence. However, this is not the case for the majority of patients, who have appeared in court for the most serious of crimes, for example, murder, manslaughter and sexual offences. The special hospital system has been the subject of a great deal of criticism and the Fallon Inquiry was the latest in a litany of official investigations into abuses of all kinds. The Fallon Inquiry investigated a series of allegations made by a patient called Stephen Doggett. Mr Doggett had absconded while on a period of escorted leave in the city centre of Liverpool. He went to Holland and forwarded a dossier to the hospital and his MP. The allegations were of an astonishing nature, including that drugs were being supplied to patients. The most serious allegation related to visits being made to

Lawrence Ward by a young girl referred to as Girl A, who was visiting a man convicted of a series of horrendous sexual offences against children. The Fallon Inquiry had a wide remit to examine the running of Lawrence Ward, as well as the treatment of personality disordered offenders and individuals in the criminal justice and psychiatric systems. The definition of personality disorder that was put to the Fallon Inquiry was as follows: 'Personality disorders are currently defined as enduring patterns of cognition, affectivity, interpersonal behaviour, impulse that are culturally deviant, pervasive and inflexible and lead to distress or social impairment' (Fallon et al, 1999: 310). This is not too far removed from Pinel's description of *manie sans délire* in 1801, which Jones (2017) describes thus: 'an individual in the grip of *manie sans délire* might not show any "change in the functions of the understanding" but instead would suffer "perversion of the active faculties, marked by sanguinary fury, with a blind propensity to acts of violence"'. The inquiry highlighted the confusions and difficulties that arose from the term. In particular, the issue of treatability was examined. Under the 1983 MHA the so-called 'treatability test' meant that those diagnosed with a personality disorder could only be detained under mental health legislation if there was evidence that the disorder was treatable in some way.

The Fallon Inquiry was unequivocal in its findings of the failings of the Ashworth regime. *The Lancet* (1999) highlighted the appalling standards of medical care and was scathing in criticisms of the psychiatrists. The inquiry found that the allegations made by Doggett in his dossier were true. These included: patients trading in pornographic material; Child A visiting convicted dangerous paedophiles and being 'groomed' for abuse while no action was taken by social workers; patients running ward businesses; and the misuse of drugs and alcohol. The inquiry recommended that Ashworth should be closed. The government did not follow that course of action; rather, the policy response to the scandal was to reform the MHA and deal with the issue of the treatability test.

The murders of Lin and Megan Russell

In July 1996, Lin Russell was walking with her children – Megan, aged six, and Josie, aged nine – in a country lane near their home in Kent when they were attacked by a man wielding a hammer. Mrs Russell and Megan died but Josie, who sustained horrific head injuries, survived and has subsequently made a dramatic recovery. Not surprisingly, the case received huge media coverage. This led to public outrage when Michael Stone, who had an extensive criminal and psychiatric history, was convicted of the murders and the assault. He was given three life sentences with a tariff of 25 years, though it is important to note that Stone has always denied any involvement in the murders. It was revealed that he had previously requested admission to detox from heroin but that this had been refused. He had also been admitted to hospital on a previous occasion but was diagnosed as a psychopath and discharged as untreatable.

Reform of the Mental Health Act

In July 1999, the Home Office and Department of Health, issued proposals concerned with the management of 'dangerous people with severe personality disorder' (DPSPD). When Home Secretary Jack Straw introduced the proposals in the House of Commons, he made specific reference to the Michael Stone case. It is a common feature of reform of the MHA that is often driven by institutional scandals or high-profile cases. This is an example where both apply. The introduction to the document argued that the vast majority of people with personality disorder cause distress to themselves and their families but do not pose a risk to the wider community. The document argued that there was a group of about 2,000 adults who would meet the criteria for the application of the proposals. It suggested that 98 per cent are men and that, at any one time, the vast majority of these individuals are in prison or special hospitals.

In the wake of the Fallon Inquiry and the Stone case, the government proposed a whole new system for the assessment and treatment of individuals diagnosed with a personality disorder and considered to pose a risk of serious violence to others (Home Office and Department of Health, 1999). The new system would involve a series of specialised units in prisons and hospitals for the evaluation and treatment of persons found to have DSPD. Following a psychiatric assessment, individuals would be transferred to a DSPD unit until the person was assessed as to be either no longer dangerous or untreatable. The majority of psychiatrists were opposed to these developments as there were serious ethical objections alongside concerns about the efficacy of the treatment regimes that would be available. Mullen (1999) argued that doctors were being asked to take on the role of judge and jailer.

Imprisonment for Public Protection

The IPP sentence was introduced in the 2003 CJA and was eventually abolished in 2012. The IPP should be placed in the context of New

Labour's general approach to penal and welfare policy. Garland (2018) noted that one feature of late modernity was a shift in the notions of rehabilitation and risk. He argued that rehabilitation came to be concerned with benefits for potential future victims rather than individual benefits for offenders. In this process, offenders and other marginalised groups are not excluded, but become subject to new strategies of social control.

The IPP sentencing provisions applied to adult offenders – a juvenile version was introduced later. The justification for the sentence was that there was a group of dangerous and violent offenders who were being released even though all the authorities knew that they continued to pose a risk to the community. The IPP sentence meant that these offenders would be given a tariff, that is, a period of time they must serve. However, they would only be released if it could be proved that they no longer posed a risk. This set up the difficult proposition of having to prove a negative. In more practical terms, the climate of risk aversion meant that it seemed virtually impossible for many offenders to demonstrate that they no longer posed the risks that had led to the imposition of the IPP. The biggest evidence against them was the offence that led to the IPP sentence in the first place. In a crowded and chaotic prison system, it became increasingly difficult for prisoners to gain access to any form of rehabilitative programme that would allow them to demonstrate some form of progress. The result was that prisoners served sentences much greater than the original tariff imposed by the trial judge. This was not just an issue of fairness and justice; additionally, the indeterminate nature of the sentence was shown to have seriously detrimental effects on the mental health of offenders and their families.

The CJA provisions applied when an offender was convicted of a 'specified' offence and was deemed to be 'dangerous'. The specified offences were listed in schedule 15 of the CJA. They included a range of sexual, violent and terrorist offences, including manslaughter, kidnapping, rape, indecency towards a child and arson. A serious offence was one that was punishable by ten or more years' imprisonment. An offender would be deemed 'dangerous' if, in the opinion of the court, 'there is significant risk to members of the public of serious harm occasioned by the commission by him of further specified offences' (CJA, 2003). In the cases of offenders under 18, similar provisions applied but the sentence was a Detention for Public Protection (DPP).

The CJA was part of the much broader New Labour project that sought to, in its own terms, restore an appropriate balance in the CJS. New Labour created the office of the Commissioner for Victims in

2004. The Halliday Report (Halliday, 2001b), *Making Punishments Work: Report of a Review of the Sentencing Framework for England & Wales*, included a wide range of proposals on sentencing. The proposals in respect of dangerous offenders were relatively modest. Dangerousness would be determined based on the risk of the offender committing future offences that would cause serious harm. This decision would be based on the pre-sentence and psychiatric reports. Halliday proposed that, in these cases, the sentence would be a determinate one. However, the offender would not be eligible for release at any stage unless the Parole Board allowed it. The sentencing court would be able to suggest that the offender would be subject to an extended period of post-release licence, which could last up to ten years. Halliday stressed that these sentencing proposals would be reserved for those offenders that posed the highest levels of risk. It recognised that the new sentence was potentially onerous and punitive.

The IPP provisions were outlined in a 2002 government White Paper, *Justice for All* (Guardian, 1999). In introducing the DSPD provisions, Straw had made specific reference to the case of Michael Stone. When discussing IPP, Straw cited the example of Roy Whiting. Whiting was convicted in 2001 of the abduction, rape and murder of an eight-year-old girl, Sarah Payne. Whiting had previously been convicted in 1995 of the abduction and sexual assault of an eight-year-old girl in 1995, and was sentenced to four years imprisonment. A psychiatric report from that time described Whiting as posing an ongoing risk to young girls. It stated that Whiting would very probably reoffend and that he might possibly kill his next victim. Whiting was released halfway through this sentence and was placed on the sex offenders register, despite his refusal to take part in sex offender programmes designed to reduce the risk of further offending.

The IPP provisions introduced by the CJA went much further than Halliday had proposed. For example, the assessment of whether an offender should be considered 'dangerous' was removed from the hands of the judge and professionals. The CJA was very prescriptive in that the court was required to assume that the defendant was 'dangerous' if they had been convicted of an offence that was listed in schedule 15. This list includes a wide range of offences, some of which, for example, affray or assault, were relatively minor compared to others on the list, such as kidnap. The result was that the 'dangerous' definition appeared to require offenders convicted of minor offences to be sentenced to either a life or IPP sentence. The result was that the CJA created something of an equivalent of the US 'three strikes and you're out' legislation, which had seen those convicted of a third felony being sentenced to life imprisonment. The IPP contributed to the rise in the prison population that took place under New Labour. In June 2008, when some changes to the IPP were introduced, there were 4,461 prisoners serving such sentences. In 2007, a Chief Inspector of Prisons report estimated that 13 per cent of IPP-sentenced prisoners had completed their minimum term. The average minimum sentence was three years but some were as little as 18 months. The short minimum IPP sentences meant that it was not possible to provide the rehabilitation that prisoners required before the term expired. This Kafkaesque situation meant that prisoners remained in detention because they could not show that the risk had diminished. The reason that they could not demonstrate this was because they had not taken part in prison rehabilitation schemes as they could not access them.

Criticism of the IPP system led to a House of Commons Justice Committee report in 2008. The committee highlighted that the IPP had made a significant contribution to prison overcrowding and was also critical of the way that the system limited judicial discretion. Finally, it suggested that IPP was a failure on its own terms as it was not targeted at the most dangerous offenders. Following this, the imposition of the IPP sentence became a decision for the sentencing judge. Despite these changes, the number of IPP-sentenced prisoners continued to grow – if there was a reduction of new sentences, there were still difficulties in releasing long-serving IPP prisoners. In 2011, there were 6,550 IPP prisoners, with 58 per cent of IPP prisoners having served longer than their minimum term. The new Coalition government produced a Green Paper suggesting reforms, including reserving IPP for the most serious offenders and reforming the test for possible release that was applied by the Parole Board. Section 123 of the Legal Aid, Sentencing, and Punishment of Offenders Act 2012(LASPO) abolished the IPP. However, it was not applied retrospectively. In 2013, the Ministry of Justice (2014) reported that there were 5,809 people in prison serving an IPP sentence; 3,570 of this group were still in prison after they had served the tariff imposed by the sentencing court. In addition, on release, IPP prisoners were subject to licence for a ten-year period. In 2016, 565 IPP prisoners were recalled – 9 per cent of the overall total of recalled prisoners. The Prison Reform Trust (2016) estimated that the cost so far of incarceration beyond tariff was in the region of £500 million.

The introduction of the IPP raised fundamental ethical questions of justice, fairness and equity. These are, of course, hugely important issues. The unjust nature of the IPP raised questions of legitimacy.

However, it is also important to consider the wider impact of the sentence on individuals, families and communities. Families and children are the forgotten victims of the penal system (Marshall, 2008). McConnell and Raikes (2019) examined the impact of IPP sentences on the families of those serving them. They make the fundamental point that all the issues that families face when a loved one is imprisoned are increased when that sentence is an IPP. These issues include social stigma, financial difficulties and the practical and emotional difficulties of maintaining a relationship. A prisoner usually has some date that they can see as the end of their sentence; however, the IPP reduces that hope for both the person serving it and their family. IPP sentences had an impact on the mental health of those serving them. The Sainsbury Centre for Mental Health (2008) reported increased rates of depression and self-harm among IPP prisoners. The Prison Reform Trust (2019) found that for every 1,000 people serving an IPP, there were 550 incidents of self-harm. In comparison, the report calculated that there were 324 incidents for people serving a determinate sentence. The rate of self-harm among IPP prisoners was twice the rate for people serving life sentences.

The introduction and use of IPP sentences crystallises many of the themes of penal and welfare policy that are examined throughout this volume. The IPP can be viewed as something of an emblematic New Labour penal measure. It was clearly meant as a signal that New Labour would keep its promise to be 'tough on crime'. It was also a complicated technocratic reform, even if the headline message was a straightforward one: we will keep dangerous people in prison and ensure that they are monitored effectively on release. Lianos and Douglas (2000) argue that modern penal policy can be viewed through a lens of what they term 'dangerisation': the tendency to see the world and individuals through a prism of danger and threat. The IPP is part of this, being the epitome of the actuarial new penology that Simon and Feeley (2003) outlined. The IPP is no longer an option for sentencing judges. However, nearly ten years after its abolition, its impacts are still being felt.

Joint enterprise

'Joint enterprise' is a legal doctrine that has developed over the past 30 years. It is discussed here because it chimes with the main themes of this chapter, which explores the impact of policies that have focused on the management of risk. These policies have also disproportionately impacted marginalised groups. This is particularly the case with joint enterprise, which has become a key element of the response to gangs and gang culture. Joint enterprise has largely been used in murder cases and has resulted in groups of young people being convicted of murder or manslaughter. For example, in 2017, seven young people were convicted of murder and four of manslaughter following the stabbing to death of Abdulwahab Hafidah in Manchester (Pidd and Perraudin, 2017). The response to gangs has disproportionately affected young people from black, Asian and minority ethnic (BAME) backgrounds.

Bridges (2013) noted that in 2012, the actions of the South African police in shooting and killing 34 miners at Marikana, and then arresting 270 other striking miners and charging them with murder, had been condemned internationally. The South African authorities had used an apartheid-era law based on a doctrine of common purpose. Common purpose had been used by the authorities to charge groups of anti-apartheid activists with the most serious of crimes. The doctrine of joint enterprise dates back to at least the mid-19th century. In its most recent modern usage, it has targeted 'gang violence'. This, in turn, has been identified as a specific problem within BAME communities. In essence, as in the death of Abdulwahab Hafidah, the doctrine holds a group of individuals responsible for the murder of an individual whatever their specific role and however marginal in the case it may have been. For example, in 2010, the Metropolitan Police produced a video entitled 'Who killed Deon?'. The video showed the murder of a young black man. A group of black youths had various roles, for example, texting messages about his whereabouts and so on. The video, which was shown in cinemas and on YouTube and Facebook, ended with the following message from the Metropolitan Police: 'If your presence, knowledge or actions lead to murder you'll be charged with murder under JE [joint enterprise].' This is a very clear and succinct summing up of the doctrine of joint enterprise. The video also sums up the concerns of campaigners against it. The message was specifically aimed at black youths and was influenced by notions of gangs and gang culture, which need to be more critically examined. Finally, it means that those with a lesser or even marginal connection to or involvement in the most serious of crimes can face the most serious charges and potentially a life sentence (Bridges, 2013).

The modern legal development of the doctrine of joint enterprise has taken place over the past 30 years or so. It can be seen as part of the broader shifts that have been discussed in this chapter: the move from a focus on individual culpability to a wider perception of the potential risks and harm, coupled with a greater concern with public protection, even if that might place individual rights at risk. Carvalho (2017a) cautions against overstating this change, arguing that there has always been a tension within the criminal law between individual rights and its function as a mechanism of social control. However, Carvalho (2017a) does acknowledge that the use of joint enterprise has created a new series of questions about the use of the law as a means of responding to social concerns about young people and violent crime. He outlines the way that joint enterprise has been heavily criticised as 'a discriminatory form of criminalisation whose wide application has tended to produce violent and exclusionary outcomes while disproportionately targeting vulnerable, marginalised and racialised populations' (Carvalho, 2017b). In the decision in the case of *R v Jogee* (2016), the Supreme Court found that the doctrine of joint enterprise had been wrongly applied for over 30 years. The facts of the case are as follows. Ameen Jogee was convicted under joint enterprise of murder in 2011. The court heard that Jogee had 'egged on' his friend, Mohammed Hirsi, who stabbed a former police officer, Paul Fyfe, in the heart. Jogee had argued that as he was not inside the house when the incident took place, he could therefore not have foreseen what his friend intended to do. Both men received life sentences for murder. This case highlighted the potential for injustice in the use of the doctrine as it is imprecise and has a range of possible applications. There are examples of cases where the notion of joint enterprise or common purpose is perhaps more clear-cut. For example, if two men plan the robbery of a shop but one acts as a lookout and the other goes in and threatens the cashier, then they will both face the same charge. Another example would be the case where an individual makes an obvious and more substantial contribution to the planning and carrying out of a crime (Krebs, 2010).

Parasitic accessorial liability (PAL) holds that an individual can be found guilty in cases where a co-defendant commits a further offence during the commission of a joint criminal enterprise. For example, if Person A plans and commits a burglary with Person B but when they break into a house, Person B assaults and murders the occupant, both would be charged with the murder. One of the fundamental problems with this doctrine is that it sets a very low threshold for culpability (Carvalho, 2017a). In the case of the use of joint enterprise, it effectively became easier to convict a group of defendants than one single defendant for the most serious of charges – murder.

At the heart of the expansion of the use of joint enterprise is a racialised 'gang discourse' (Williams and Clarke, 2016). The 'gang discourse' is the latest manifestation of racialised discourses of crime (Hall et al, 2013; Gilroy, 1982, 2013). Williams and Clarke (2016) argue that the current discourse is heavily influenced by US notions of law enforcement and responses to youth crime. At the time of writing, the protests against the murder of George Floyd and the wider Black Lives Matter movement seem to indicate that the underlying notions that underpin these responses are beginning to unravel. However, there is clearly a danger that there will be the emergence of a stronger state as right-wing politicians become more authoritarian and play to an older, whiter electoral base. Williams and Clarke (2016) see the Metropolitan Police's Operation Trident in 1998 and Greater Manchester Police's Manchester Action Against Guns and Gangs in 2001 as the start of US-style 'war on gangs'. The danger of such initiatives is that they reproduce and reinforce, rather than challenge, a series of racist stereotypes.

The role of gangs in the 2011 riots was limited. However, the media and the Coalition sought to portray gangs as the organisers. Following the riots, the Home Office introduced the Ending Gangs and Youth Violence initiative, which has echoes of the Troubled Families initiative (Crossley, 2016). A total of £10 million was made available in 2012–3 to support mainstream services to identify young people 'at risk' of becoming involved in gangs or other forms of violence. To receive funding, local authorities had to demonstrate that a 'gang problem' existed in their area. In Manchester, areas of the city with higher BAME populations were more likely to be identified as having a 'gang problem' (Williams and Clarke, 2016).

There is a fundamental issue at the heart of this approach: the notion of the gang. The media representation of a gang as a well-organised group is somewhat at odds with the reality, particularly in the case of young people. In some of the joint enterprise cases, groups of school friends were being portrayed as gang members rather than a much looser association of friends and acquaintances. The powerful gang narrative helped shape the development of the prosecution case, so sharing text messages or videos online were all viewed through the prism of a wider developing criminal conspiracy that led to a murder. There is, of course, no clear definition of gang membership and gangs do not have lists of members. Joint enterprise became a key element in the response to the issue of young people and violent crime. Proving that a defendant was a member of a gang was often crucial to the case. Alongside this, in many of the cases, such as the murder of Abdulwahab Hafidah, gang rivalry was a key element in the construction of the prosecution case. Williams and Clarke (2016) show that rap videos, tattoos and so on were all used as either signs of gang affiliation or, more broadly, 'bad character'. This is not to suggest that elements of this did not take place, but rather to highlight the way that the prosecution in these cases broadened the scope of involvement.

The media reporting of these cases used a deeply racialised and dehumanising language that is an example of dog-whistle politics (Haney-López, 2014). In newspaper reports of these crimes, young people were frequently referred to as 'packs of wolves', 'animals', 'baying for blood' and 'hunting their victims'. Such terms reinforce the gang discourse and play on deeply entrenched and long-standing racist constructions of 'black criminality'. When researchers interviewed prisoners who had been sentenced under joint enterprise, 45 per cent had not been present at the scene of the crime for which they were convicted and the majority did not see themselves as gang members.

The gang discourse also plays into a wider discourse of 'territorial stigmatisation' (Wacquant, 2007). In modern usage, the term 'ghetto' suggests an area of poor housing, poverty, substance misuse problems, high crime and gang violence; however, it also has racist overtones. More recently in the UK, governments of all political persuasions have been concerned with the issue of so-called 'problem' or 'sink' estates. Young people who live in neighbourhoods that are experiencing high crime rates will grow up with, go to school with and have contact with others who become involved in gangs. McKenzie's (2015) portrait of life on a Nottingham estate – *Getting By* – focuses not only on the economic and social pressures facing the residents, but also on the ways in which they overcome them. McKenzie (2015) notes that part of the response to this vilification is that people assert the positive aspects of the area and their connections with it. This can clearly have negative effects as the notions of territory, and disputes about it, are key in the construction of the gang discourse.

One of the major criticisms of joint enterprise is that it lowered the standard of proof that was required to secure a conviction for the most serious of crimes – it came to be used almost exclusively in murder cases. In these cases, it is clear that, as in the Jogee case, the level of culpability can vary enormously between defendants. However, the whole premise of joint enterprise removes these sorts of questions. The jury may have doubts about individual roles and culpabilities but they are instructed to reach a verdict on the basis of the whole group. The House of Commons Justice Committee (2012), in its report on joint enterprise, was critical of the lack clarity in such an important area of law. In addition, the report was concerned by the type and standard of evidence used, the effective lowering of the standard of proof, and the number of claims of injustice that were related to the doctrine. Krebs (2010) argued that joint enterprise had become a 'lazy law', which was used in the most serious cases and overwhelmingly favoured the prosecution. In such cases, large numbers of people may be arrested on suspicion of involvement in the most serious crimes. The construction of the prosecution case is often largely based on association, which places individuals at risk of facing a life sentence for limited involvement in the actual physical act of murder.

The whole-life sentence

The development of the whole-life sentence is inextricably linked with the case of Myra Hindley – the Moors Murderer – so I will briefly outline that case. Hindley's pleas to the Parole Board and the official responses to it led to the creation of the whole-life tariff. The high-profile nature of Hindley's case is an important factor. In addition, the wider concerns about increases in violent crime and the media fascination with the figure of the serial killer combined to influence penal policy and sentencing. There are around 70 whole-life tariff prisoners who have been told that they will never be released from custody. This is a small fraction of the prison population in England and Wales; in the US, around 50,000 prisoners are serving such sentences. The numbers may be small but such sentences clearly raise hugely important ethical and moral questions. In addition, as Simon (2010b) notes, the sentence for murder has an important impact on the severity of punishment for all crime, particularly serious crime.

Serial killing, modernity and the Moors Murders

In 1966, Brady and Hindley were convicted of the abduction, sexual assault and murder of Lesley Ann Downey (aged ten), John Kilbride (aged 12) and Edward Evans (aged 17). Lesley Ann Downey's and John Kilbride's bodies were buried on Saddleworth Moor outside of Manchester. The 'Moors Murders', as the case became known, was the most high-profile murder case in Britain in the 20th century. Two other children, Pauline Reade (aged 16) and Keith Bennett (aged 12), had gone missing in Manchester in the period when Hindley and Brady had committed these murders. It was always felt that Pauline Reade and Keith Bennett had been victims of the Moors Murderers, but despite a huge search, their bodies were not found in the initial investigation of the case. In 1985, Brady and Hindley eventually confessed to the murders of Pauline Reade and Keith Bennett. In a huge police operation, they were taken back to the Moors in an attempt to find the missing bodies. Pauline Reade was found but, at the time of writing, the body of Keith Bennett has never been found.

Bauman (2007: 117) suggested that modern society is based on 'disengagement, discontinuity and forgetting', which are features of responses to representations of crime and violence. Serial killing is a phenomenon of modernity as it is associated with the rise of the urban 'society of strangers'. The killer usually has no relationship of any kind with the victims and, unlike other such crimes, which take place in the context of a relationship or as a result of a feud, the murders are instrumental. Thus, serial killing can be seen as something of a symbol of the loss of notions of community (Haggerty, 2009). Another key feature of modernity is the role of the mass media and the rise of celebrity culture. There is a symbiotic relationship between the media and serial killers (Cummins et al, 2019). Clark (2011) examines the case in the context of the sociological literature on evil, an area of sociology that has recently begun to expand, and the processes resulting in Hindley becoming the 'most hated woman in Britain'.

Brady and Hindley were sentenced to life imprisonment in May 1966. The trial was the first high-profile case following the abolition of the death penalty. The vote in the House of Commons on the abolition took place while Brady and Hindley were on remand awaiting trial. The murders they committed all took place when the death penalty was in force. If they had been arrested earlier, they would almost certainly have been executed. When the death penalty was abolished, it was not the intention that it would be replaced by a whole-life sentence. The trial judge set a tariff and when the offender had served that period, they would be able to appeal to the Parole Board. If this appeal was successful, they would be released under life licence – in effect, a form of parole – for the rest of their lives. The trial judge, in line with the wider social views of the time, saw Hindley as having come under Brady's influence. He suggested that, away from Brady's influence, there was potential for her to reform and be rehabilitated. Brady never applied for parole at any point and, under the MHA, was transferred to Ashworth Special Hospital in the 1980s because he was assessed as being mentally ill.

Hindley's campaign for parole was given very visible and high-profile public support, most notably, by Lord Longford. This was particularly the case before her confession to the murders of Pauline Reade and Keith Bennett. During her later time in prison, Hindley was something of a 'model prisoner', even completing an Open University degree. In reports to the Parole Board, she was viewed as being at low risk of offending on release. There would have clearly been risks in her being released, both potential risks to her safety and clear political risks – it would have been a very brave Home Secretary indeed who signed her release forms. Hindley never escaped from her crimes and the famous photograph taken of her when she was arrested in 1965 (Cummins et al, 2019). Pettigrew (2016: 99) concluded that 'The combination of gender, sexualised murder, and child victims, in the public mind, placed Hindley beyond any notion of rehabilitation, beyond anything that could make her comprehensible'. Hindley made a number of appeals to the Home Secretary requesting confirmation of how long she would have to serve before being eligible for parole. These included legal representations arguing for a determinate sentence to be imposed. These failed and Hindley sought a judicial review of the tariff and the basis for converting the whole-life tariff to a determinate sentence (Schone, 2000). The Home Secretary's decision to impose the whole-life tariff to a determinate period would only be made on the basis of retribution and deterrence, not the overall progress of a prisoner. The progress that Hindley had made in prison was thus excluded and the Home Secretary would not take into consideration her behaviour and achievements while incarcerated.

Michael Howard's treatment of Hindley was found to be unlawful because she should have been informed that he had decided that a whole-life tariff had been imposed and the reason for making that decision. The failings in this legal process were rectified by changes introduced by New Labour's first Home Secretary, Jack Straw. These changes allowed for the consideration of exceptional progress made by a prisoner when considering changes to the tariff (Pettigrew, 2016). Straw agreed with Howard's decision for a whole-life tariff, which created the possibility of an appeal of the grounds of exceptional progress. Hindley's appeals against the whole-life tariff were considered again by the Court of Appeal and the whole-life tariff was considered to be lawful. This decision focused on the decision-making process but the court did raise concerns about the nature of the whole-life tariff (Schone, 2000). In rejecting Hindley's application for a judicial review of the whole-life tariff, one argument put forward by Judge Steyn of the Divisional Court was that Hindley's and Brady's crimes were 'uniquely evil'. However, this is clearly not the case as others have committed such sadistic murders.

While accepting that the Hindley case was the hardest of hard cases, Schone, (2000) argued that there had been an abdication of the rule of law. The decisions around the questions about parole and the length of the tariff were political. Given Hindley's tabloid status as the 'most evil woman in Britain', as well as the media interest in the case, it was highly unlikely that she would have ever been paroled. However, this does not mean that the case for parole should not have been considered. Hindley eventually accepted that she would remain in prison. She died in prison in November 2002; by that time, she was the longest-serving prisoner, having been in custody for 37 years.

The 2003 Criminal Justice Act

Pettigrew (2016) describes Hindley as the unwitting architect of the whole-life tariff. Her various appeals had demonstrated the inconsistencies in not only the decision-making process, but also the role of the home secretary. For offenders aged under 18, a decision by the ECHR in the Bulger case had stripped the home secretary of the power to set a tariff and a similar decision followed in the case of Anthony Anderson. Anderson was a convicted double murderer who had been sentenced to life imprisonment in 1988, with the judge placing the tariff at 15 years. This was then raised to 20 by the Home Secretary. Anderson won his case in the House of Lords that this was a breach of his human rights as he had been denied the opportunity to contest the increased sentence. The government appealed but the decision was upheld in the ECHR. As a result, politicians could no longer decide if or when a prisoner should be considered for parole. When sentencing an individual to life imprisonment, the judge sets a minimum term. This can only be amended by the Court of Appeal or the Supreme Court. However, the attorney general, a political figure, can legally challenge sentences that they consider to be too lenient.

The 2003 CJA introduced the current framework for the sentencing of offenders who receive a life sentence. Judges are required to give reasons in court if they depart from the guidance outlined in the CJA. The guidelines state that multiple murderers – offenders who murder two or more people – should receive a whole-life term where these crimes involved sexual abuse, preplanning, abduction or terrorism. The abduction and murder of a single child or a child murder that involves sexual assault or sadism also requires a whole-life sentence under the CJA guidelines. Under these guidelines, Brady and Hindley would have both received whole-life terms. Since 2015, the murder of a police or prison officer during the course of their duty also leads to a whole-life term. Offenders who commit a murder in the furtherance of a political, religious or ideological cause will also receive a whole-life term. If any offender commits a second murder after having been previously convicted of one, they will receive a whole-life sentence. After any appeals, whole-life sentences are then only subject to further review on compassionate grounds – a power that has never been used.

Simon (2010b: 1310), in highlighting the potential inflationary impact of sentences for murder, concludes that 'where punishments are extreme, there is the potential and perhaps inexorable pull toward more severe punishment for all'. This has been the case in England and Wales, which saw a doubling of the prison population in a 20-year period from the early 1990s. The Prison Reform Trust (2018) reported that there were 8,554 inmates across the UK serving life sentences. This figure is higher than France, Germany and Italy combined. One of the aspects of short -term populist penal policies is that the longer-term impacts are not fully considered. This is a case in point, with the Prison Reform Trust highlighting that life-sentenced prisoners in the UK make up more than 10 per cent of the total prison population and are a significant factor in the wider prison crisis.

Conclusion

New Labour was not totally responsible for all the shifts in policy that have been discussed in this chapter, which are linked by a strong number of factors. The first is the sense that the CJS and agencies within it had become too focused on the needs of individual offenders rather than the needs of victims and wider society. Linked to this is a common populist notion that rather than fighting the war on crime, the CJS was being led by a liberal elite whose policies tied the hands of the police and the courts. As has been emphasised, New Labour was determined not to be politically outflanked on the issue of law and order. However, these policies were not solely the result of cynical political manoeuvring; rather, it is argued here that they reflect the core communitarianism of New Labour thinking. What links these developments is a sense of othering. These changes not only had an impact on longer sentences for individuals, but also added to the narrative that the CJS was failing to protect the most vulnerable and that this failure was the result of liberal penal policy.

7

Austerity and the Big Society

Introduction

The obituary of David Cameron's political career will inevitably focus on his decision to hold a referendum on the UK's membership of the EU. After the referendum in June 2016 and the vote to leave, Cameron resigned. The aftermath of the Brexit vote and the ongoing political disruption will be the subject of debate and analysis for the foreseeable future. This chapter will not be exploring these issues; instead, it will focus on Cameron's domestic policies in the period 2010–16. The most significant of these policies was austerity. 'Austerity' is the name given to the combination of the reduction in public services and welfare retrenchment that was followed by the Coalition government from 2010 onwards. Austerity and its impact are discussed in depth in the following. In the area of domestic politics, one of the most significant events was the riots of 2011, which are examined later. The chapter begins with a discussion of Cameron's key political idea: the Big Society. This encapsulates Cameron's attempts to reduce the role of the state while, at the same time, reinvigorating community groups. It can be read as a combination of modernising tendencies and nostalgic notions of community and civic involvement. One of the key issues in the Brexit referendum was immigration. Cameron, alongside his Home Secretary and successor, Theresa May, had responded to the issue of immigration by creating a 'hostile environment' for illegal immigrants. When he was elected Conservative leader in 2005, he presented himself as a reforming moderniser, being socially liberal but economically conservative. There is clearly a tension between these two poles. In the areas of welfare and penal policy, particularly in response to the 2011 riots, Cameron tacked to the right.

The Big Society

> You can call it liberalism. You can call it empowerment.
> You can call it freedom. You can call it responsibility. I call
> it the Big Society. The Big Society is about a huge culture
> change – where people ... don't always turn to officials,
> local authorities or central government for answers to the
> problems they face but instead feel both free and powerful
> enough to help themselves and their own communities.
> (Cameron, 2010)

North (2011) notes that it is easy to be cynical about Cameron's notion
of the Big Society. Its critics see it as a cover for the reduction in the
public sector and withdrawal of services. However, it is important to
examine it on its own terms. In a series of speeches, Cameron put
forward his analysis of the causes of what he termed 'Broken Britain'.
The features of Cameron's Broken Britain are a familiar litany of the
Right's criticisms of the failings of the welfare state and the alleged
social pathologies it creates: worklessness, unemployment, anti-social
behaviour, lack of parental responsibility and single-parent families.
Cameron was seen by many as very close in social policy terms to Blair;
however, he was highly critical of New Labour. Cameron argued that
the social-democratic Fabianism of New Labour had failed in two ways.
First, the size of the state had increased, which had an inhibiting impact
on community-based initiatives and social action. Cameron argued
that what he saw as the expansion of the state under New Labour had
promoted selfishness and individualism rather than social solidarity.
There is something of a contradiction here as one might expect
Cameron to be in favour of increased individualism. The Big Society
was Cameron's attempt to resolve these apparently contradictory trends.
Norman (2010) produced an influential, in Conservative circles, book
that presented the Big Society as an alternative to what he argued
was the centralism and managerialism of the Blair and Brown years.
Norman (2010) outlined a number of examples of late 19th-century
and early 20th-century working-class organisations – building societies,
cooperatives and insurance societies – that were forms of social action
that did not involve the state.

Larner (2003) argues that there is a danger of seeing neoliberalism
as a meta-narrative. Part of the danger with this is that it ignores
or obscures the difficulties that went before. The centralising and
managerialist tendencies in the public services in the New Labour
period did have a negative impact on both the delivery of services

and the morale of workers in the public sector. When the state is over-dominant, it is important to produce a critique of its impact (Tam, 2011). There is, of course, a history of anti-statism on the Left that would chime with a number of the themes of the Big Society. This would include examples of community-based self-help initiatives such as credit unions. These examples are used to demonstrate that not all self-help is necessarily rooted in neo-conservative anti-statist ideologies. Having acknowledged that, it was clear that the Big Society uncritically accepted long-standing Conservative prejudices of an overly bureaucratic state. Alongside this, the private and third sectors were seen as more efficient and responsive to community needs, and there was a final assumption that volunteers and philanthropy would have the capacity to replace state services or develop new ones. However, this is in the context of the UK, which is a very centralised state.

National Citizen Service

Cameron's mixture of modernisation and traditional Conservative values is very evident in the establishment of the National Citizen Service (NCS). Traditional Tories have long been concerned about what they see as a decline in social cohesion. They link this to broader concerns about the influence of progressive ideas and approaches in education, which are seen as producing a decline in not only educational standards, but also wider behaviour. One response is to call for the return of National Service. The National Service Act 1948 established that all healthy males aged 17 to 21 had to undertake an 18-month period of duty in the forces. They then remained on the reserve list for four years. National Service was effectively abolished at the beginning of the 1960s. Social conservatives have a nostalgic view of it instilling discipline, a sense of duty and patriotism. In 2007, the Conservative Party produced a policy document that proposed a school-leaver programme that 'will help young people to develop a sense of purpose, optimism and belonging which will reduce their desire to binge drink, carry weapons and take drugs. It will be a positive and potent weapon to tackle anti-social behaviour' (Conservatives, 2007: 1). The idea for the NCS was coupled with Cameron's vision of the Big Society (Mycock and Tonge, 2011; Mohan, 2012). The scheme was further highlighted after the 2011 riots. The NCS programme begins with groups of teenagers undertaking a residential visit, usually in an outdoor education-style centre. It involves physical and team-building activities, which are common across other areas, including management and leadership courses. The alleged 'character-building' aspect of such activities is a deeply engrained cultural trope. This is then followed by a residential phase where the NCS recruits experience independent living, with the aim of developing a variety of skills for their future.

In the third phase, the NCS recruits plan and deliver a 'social action' project in their local community. It costs £50 to take part in the scheme and when NCS recruits complete the course, there is a graduation ceremony in which NCS graduates receive a certificate signed by the Prime Minister. Underpinning the NCS was a particularly Conservative notion of the 'active citizen'. The NCS graduate is presented as a counterpoint or alternative to the alleged apathetic teenager who is 'at risk' of becoming involved in crime or anti-social behaviour. No one seriously doubts the need to provide constructive activities and opportunities for young people on the verge of early adulthood. However, this scheme was introduced at a time when youth and community services were experiencing significant retrenchment. In addition, there is a certain irony in the fact that the flagship scheme of the Big Society was the creation of central government.

The NCS has somewhat faded from public view but can be seen as an attempt by the Cameron government to combine the traditionalist and modernising trends within its social programme. If one looks past the brochures and advertising that gave it something of modern feel, it is actually a combination of very traditional Conservative approaches. It focuses on 'character building', which is achieved by a series of physical activities and social action. It was also imbued with patriotic values, which presents a very particular and problematic view of British history. In a speech to the Conservative Party conference in October 2015, Cameron stated:

> 'I want my children – I want all our children to know they're part of something big – the proudest multi-racial democracy on earth. That's why we're making sure they learn British history at school. That's why we started National Citizen Service to bring different people together. I want them to grow up proud of our country.' (Cameron, 2015b)

As noted earlier, NCS recruits had to pay a fee to take part in the programme. Even though bursaries were available, this inevitably excluded some groups. NCS graduates were primarily from middle-class families. Ipsos MORI's (2015) evaluation of the 2014 scheme found that only 20 per cent were eligible for free school meals and itt had on average far more female (71 per cent) than male participants.

Troubled families

Like Thatcher, Major and Blair before him, Cameron was clearly influenced by and accepted a great deal of Murray's (1990) underclass discourse. Welshman (2013) shows that the underclass discourse is a modern recasting of long-standing tropes. These portray the poorest as 'other', set apart geographically, socially and even psychologically from the wider society (Cummins, 2018). The influence of Murray's underclass discourse on Cameron is perhaps most apparent in the response to the 2011 riots and the development of the Troubled Families programme. The Troubled Families agenda has its origins in the New Labour government's 2006 Respect agenda. This claimed to identify a small group of families who were a drain on public services, including health, social services, education and the police. As Cameron put it: 'Whatever you call them, we've known for years that a relatively small number of families are the source of a large proportion of the problems in society. Drug addiction. Alcohol abuse. Crime. A culture of disruption and irresponsibility that cascades through generations.' (Cameron, 2015b). The Respect agenda, despite its moralising title, did at least focus on multiple disadvantages, such as low income and poor housing (Crossley, 2015). However, the Troubled Families policy abandoned this. It was claimed that there were 120,000 such families and that various government agencies spend £9 billion a year responding to the social problems that they created.

The national Troubled Families initiative was a multi-agency approach to supporting families. Multi-agency approaches were at the core of both New Labour and Big Society initiatives. The aim of the Troubled Families policy was to 'turn around' the most chaotic and challenging families within the county. In doing so, it would improve family and community outcomes, as well as reduce the demand on public sector services. A troubled family was defined as one where five out of the seven forms of deprivation were present:

- no parent in the family is in work;
- the family lives in overcrowded housing;
- no parent has any qualifications;
- the mother has mental health problems;
- at least one parent has a long-standing limiting illness, disability or infirmity;
- the family has a low income (below 60 per cent of median income);
- the family cannot afford a number of food and clothing items.

The Department for Communities and Local Government (DCLG, 2012) suggested that troubled families are those that:

- are involved in crime or anti-social behaviour;
- have children who are regularly truanting or not attending school;
- have an adult on out-of-work benefits;
- have domestic violence and abuse;
- have homelessness/housing issues;
- have health problems, for example, mental health and drug/alcohol misuse issues;
- do not take up early years entitlements;
- have child protection issues;
- cost the public sector large sums in responding to their problems.

The Troubled Families funding was on a payment-by-results basis and local authorities were given target numbers for the troubled families living in their areas. Given the funding mechanisms, it is perhaps not too surprising that they appeared remarkably successful in identifying these families. Levitas (2012) outlines the porous nature of categories: a 'family with troubles' quickly becomes a 'troubled family'. In her discussion of similar policy developments in New Zealand, Beddoe (2014) notes that these shifts have taken place at a time of cuts and retrenchment in the welfare budget. The Troubled Families approach can best be described as nonsense or tough love. It was embodied in the figure of the leader of the programme, Louise Casey. Casey cultivated an image as a straight talker who was determined to shake up the complacency of the liberal elite, which she saw as dominating family policy. This was music to the ears of the Cameron government. The internal evaluation of the Troubled Families scheme was overwhelmingly positive, stating that as a result of targeted Troubled Families interventions, children were back in school, adults were in employment or on a path back to work, and youth crime and anti-social behaviour had been reduced. The evaluation claimed that the Troubled Families programme had saved taxpayers an estimated £1.2 billion, from a maximum government investment of £448 million. It stated that the average gross cost saving to the taxpayer per troubled family was £12,000, with the average cost of the programme's intervention being £5,493. For example, in Manchester, for every £1 invested in the programme, £2.20 in gross benefits had been realised. These figures would mean that the Troubled Families programme was one of the most successful social programmes in post-war Britain, having a positive impact on 88 per cent of the 120,000 'troubled families' in the country. An independent evaluation was much more circumspect, stating that 'across a wide range of outcomes, covering the key objectives of the programme – employment, benefit receipt, school attendance, safeguarding and child welfare – we were unable to find consistent evidence that the troubled families programme had any significant or systematic impact' (Department for Communities and Local Government, 2016).

The 2011 riots

In August 2011, there was a series of disturbances across major cities in England. The riots began in London when, on 4 August 2011, the police shot dead Mark Duggan. The background to the case has been very controversial. Duggan, aged 29, was shot by police officers who intercepted a minicab in which he was travelling. An inquest jury found that Duggan was not holding a weapon when he was shot; however, it concluded that he had been lawfully killed. Duggan's family challenged this verdict but both the High Court and the Court of Appeal ruled against them, and the Supreme Court declined to hear the case. The family have lodged an appeal with the ECHR, but in October 2019, the Metropolitan Police reached a confidential settlement with the Duggan family. On 6 August 2011, there was a demonstration outside the local police station in Tottenham. While this was initially a peaceful demonstration, as frustration grew, disorder developed. This then spread across London and on to Birmingham, Manchester, Salford, Nottingham and Liverpool.

Benyon (2012) argues that radical perspectives see rioting as purposeful action with a political meaning – the so-called 'ballot box of the poor'. While decrying the damage that riots cause, a centrist/liberal position regards them as inevitable in circumstances of widespread social deprivation. Conservatives see riots as wanton vandalism, a social outrage carried out by criminal elements and potentially organised and exploited by political extremists. In this view, rioters are mindless criminals and dupes. The different perspectives lead to calls for different responses. Both the liberal and radical perspectives suggest that the solutions lie in changing the social conditions that have led to the riots. The Conservative response focuses on the need for a strong state – the apprehending of offenders and the imposition of long sentences to act as a deterrent to further rioting. Cameron and London Mayor Boris Johnson were out of the country on holiday when the riots occurred.

After the first day of rioting in London, there was unusual criticism of the police for losing control. In response, the Metropolitan Police Service launched a huge operation that saw the deployment of officers at potential hotspots. On 11 August 2011, there was a parliamentary debate on the riots. The conservative (not party-political) perspective was dominant. Cameron described the riots as 'criminality pure and simple'. Hazel Blears, Labour MP for Salford, stated that the disturbances were 'deliberate, organised, violent criminality'. Theresa May, then Home Secretary, concluded that the 'vast majority were not protesting they were thieving'. The Justice Secretary, Ken Clarke, in a nod to the influence of Murray, described the riots as the product of a 'feral underclass'. There were some who departed from this line and presented a liberal perspective, asking questions about the social conditions that produced the riots. Ed Miliband, leader of the opposition, questioned why the rioters felt that they had nothing to lose. David Lammy, the MP for Tottenham, suggested that the riots indicated that there had been a polarisation not between black and white, a feature of previous urban disturbances, but between those with a stake in society and those without.

Riots and urban disturbances have been a reoccurring feature of modern political history. Waddington (1992) divides rioting in Britain from 1900 onwards into broad phases. It should be noted here that this does not include rioting and urban disturbances that took place as part of the Civil Rights movement or the Troubles in Northern Ireland. Waddington (1992) characterised the riots between 1900 and 1962 as 'interracial', that is, attacks on immigrant communities. An example of this would be the Notting Hill and Nottingham 'race riots' in 1958 (Pilkington, 1988). The 1970s saw riots in Lewisham and Southall following anti-fascist demonstrations. The Southall riot that saw the death of anti-fascist activist Blair Peach took place after protesters gathered to demonstrate against a National Front campaign meeting. There were also riots in the 1970s that were primarily confrontations between marginalised and disenfranchised black youths and police.

In the urban disturbances of the 1980s that took place in London, Bristol, Manchester and Liverpool, race was clearly a factor (Newburn, 2014). In all these areas, long-standing issues, including racial discrimination, poor housing and high levels of unemployment among black youth, were compounded by discriminatory policing. For example, the Brixton Riot of 1981 was, in part, triggered by Operation Swamp. It is a minor point but it seems quite staggering to think that such an operation could have such a racially intensive title. Operation Swamp 81 began in April 1981 and saw the intensive use of stop-and-search powers under the Vagrancy Act – popularly known as the Sus Laws. These powers were used disproportionately against black youths. In 1985, there was another riot in Brixton following the death of Cherry Groce. Mrs Groce was shot by the police in an armed raid on her property while attempting to arrest her son. The Broadwater Farm Riot of 1985, which saw the murder of PC Keith Blakelock, was triggered by the death of Cynthia Jarrett, who died in disputed circumstances when the police were searching her home.

The Brixton Riot of 1981 was followed three months later by riots in Liverpool, Manchester, Bristol and Leeds. The factors that provoked these disturbances were very similar to those in Brixton, being a combination of poverty, urban deprivation and the over-policing of people of colour. Scarman (1981) concluded that racial discrimination and disadvantage had been key factors in the riot. He also called for action to tackle the fact that the police had become distant from the communities they served. Part of this action would require the recruitment of more black police officers. He concluded that 'urgent action' was needed to prevent racial disadvantage becoming an 'endemic, ineradicable disease threatening the very survival of our society' (Scarman, 1981). One notable feature of the government's response to the 2011 riots was a refusal to consider the establishment of a Scarman-style public inquiry. Looking back at the responses to the riots of the early 1980s, there seems to have been much more sympathy for the liberal perspective. Scarman (1981) openly highlighted the social factors and actions of the police as causes of the riots. This is not to say that there were not commentators and politicians who did not dismiss the riots as criminality pure and simple. In 2015, a memo about the riot was released under the 30-years rule. It was written by Oliver Letwin, now an MP but then working as an advisor to Mrs Thatcher. It presented a deeply racist perspective on the causes of the riot, alongside a nostalgic view of Britain during the Depression:

> Lower-class, unemployed white people lived for years in appalling slums without a breakdown of public order on anything like the present scale; in the midst of the depression, people in Brixton went out, leaving their grocery money in a bag at the front door, and expecting to see groceries there when they got back. ... Riots, criminality and social disintegration are caused solely by individual characters and attitudes. So long as bad moral attitudes remain, all efforts to improve the inner cities will founder. (Kirkup and Winnett, 2012)

The responses to the 2011 riots were of a different nature to those in the early 1980s as they were presented or seen as apolitical – almost a form of consumerism. The fact that shops selling phones, computers, other electrical goods, clothing and trainers were targeted was used as evidence that this was not a form of political protest, but a consumer binge by those who were otherwise excluded from the delights of modern capitalism (Bauman, 2011; Zizek, 2011; Harvey, 2012). This produced the rather odd spectacle of a form of nostalgia for politically motivated rioting.

Newburn (2014) argues that this focus on the alleged consumerist attitudes of rioters needs to be approached in a much more careful fashion. In one form or another, looting is a feature of virtually all urban disturbances. The London School of Economics and Political Science (LSE), in conjunction with *The Guardian*, carried out the most detailed research with those who took part in the 2011 riots (Lewis et al, 2011). The project interviewed 270 people: 80 per cent were male; 30 per cent were juveniles aged 10–17 and 49 per cent were aged 18–25; and 26 per cent were white, 47 per cent were black and 5 per cent were Asian. From an analysis of court records, the project concluded that 59 per cent of the rioters came from the 20 per cent of the most deprived areas in the UK; only 3 per cent of the rioters came from the richest areas. The project notes that there were significant differences between London and the rest of the country. In London, 32 per cent of those involved were white; this contrasts with Liverpool, where 79 per cent of the rioters were white, and Salford and Manchester, where the rioters were overwhelmingly white. A total of 81 per cent of the rioters thought that riots would occur again. The causes of the riots were identified as relations with the police, stop and search, the role of gangs and the Blackberry messaging system (BBM). Those involved in the riots clearly stated that the role of gangs was totally overplayed. Cameron and other politicians claimed that the gangs had a key role in organising the riots; however, those involved stated that the most significant intervention by the gangs was to hold a truce. In the interviews, those who had taken part in the riots identified the grievances that caused the riots as the scrapping of the Educational Maintenance Allowance (EMA), tuition fees, the closure of youth services and the shooting of Mark Duggan. The first three were all introduced as part of austerity measures. Young people were disproportionately targeted in these policies, with 73 per cent of those interviewed as part of the project having been stopped and searched. The shooting of Duggan seemed to have a symbolic value of the treatment to which they felt that they were subject. 'Reading the riots' (Lewis et al, 2011) highlights the disaffection that those involved in the riots felt: only 14 per cent strongly agreed with the statement 'I feel that I am part of British society'.

After the initial show of force, the police carried out a huge operation to track down and convict those involved in rioting. The rise of CCTV and social media meant that many of the acts had been filmed and it was fairly easy to identify the culprits. Some magistrates' courts introduced all-night and weekend sittings to process the number of cases that were before them. The Head of the Crown Prosecution Service, Alison Saunders, even appeared in court to prosecute cases. This was clearly a symbolic gesture but it was significant – a statement of the nature of the response. Not only was justice dispensed quickly, but sentencing was also harsher. Nearly 1,300 people were jailed for their part in the rioting, with the average custodial sentence being 16.8 months. Two men from Cheshire were jailed for four years each after admitting an offence of inciting disorder, though none actually resulted. They had posted on Facebook a notice of a 'Smash Down Northwich Town' event. This encouraged people to meet behind a McDonalds in the town centre during the afternoon of 9 August. The police actually attended but no rioters materialised.

The 1981 versus 2011 riots

The response to the 2011 riots was to couch them largely in terms of the need for increased and more effective police but there was no official Scarman-style inquiry into the causes. The political response to rioting is usually unequivocal in its support of the police. However, as noted earlier, this was not the case in 2011. The Home Affairs Select Committee conducted an inquiry and found that police tactics had failed, which had allowed rioting to spread. One of the most significant differences between 1981 and 2011 is the fact that the conservative perspective was more deeply entrenched, both in media and in political circles. The rioters of 2011 were ironically seen as too deeply enmeshed in consumerism. While structural and institutional racism had been acknowledged as a cause of the riots of the early 1980s, it was notable by its absence in the wider discourse. It did appear in a rant by David Starkey – a historian of Tudor England, not a sociologist or criminologist – who claimed 'the whites have become black', attacking a 'destructive, nihilistic gangster culture' that he claimed had become the 'fashion' (BBC, 2011). Starkey had become a public figure as a panelist on Radio 4's The Moral Maze. He had gained a reputation for making provocative and controversial statements, so it is tempting to dismiss his rant given this context. However, the wider reactions to the 2011 riots demonstrate the way that some of the key notions of Murray's underclass discourse had become deeply entrenched within the political discourse.

What is striking about the riots of the early 1980s and 2011 are the similarities. The 2011 riots were not some new form of anarchic consumerism. Benyon (2012) highlights the interrelated factors that contribute to the potential for riots, which include:

- High unemployment – this has a particular impact on young people who will find it more difficult to gain access to the labour market and well-paid work.
- Poverty and poor housing – these are linked to other factors, including low educational attainment and the lack of youth services. The EMA paid young people from poorer backgrounds aged 16–18 an allowance of £30 a week if they were in full-time education. Its abolition, along with cuts to youth services, was one of the first acts of austerity.
- Racial disadvantage and discrimination.
- Political exclusion.
- Mistrust of the police – the findings of the Scarman Report (Scarman, 1981) on this issue were almost replicated in 'Reading the riots' (Lewis et al, 2011).

The hostile environment

In 2013, the Home Secretary, Theresa May, announced that she was going to introduce a new approach to immigration. The specific aim of this policy would be to create a 'really hostile environment for illegal immigrants' (York, 2018). This was something of a departure in being such an explicit statement. However, there were clear continuities with New Labour's general approach to immigration and asylum. The term 'hostile environment' had previously been used by Labour ministers; however, it came into much wider use in this period. One of the features of the shift towards right-wing populist politics has been the conflation of anti-immigrant and anti-welfare policies. This produces the strange phenomenon of 'Schrodinger's immigrant': immigrants are portrayed as both moving to take jobs from British workers while, at the same time, defrauding the welfare system. This is a modern formulation of long-standing tropes that immigrants to the UK have faced.

The notion of the 'hostile environment' is based on the premise that the UK has always provided a warm welcome to immigrants whatever their background. In addition, implicit in the term is the idea that the current system is being exploited and that the UK is a 'soft touch'. At best, this is a rather naive and simplistic view of British history. In the post-war period, Irish, Caribbean and Asian immigrants had faced racism and discrimination, including frequent calls for repatriation (Wills, 2017; Hirsch, 2018). Anti-immigrant sentiment had been fuelled by the tabloid media. The issue was ultimately to play a key role in the EU referendum campaign as anti-immigrant sentiment was exploited by Nigel Farage and the Leave campaign. This culminated in the Vote Leave campaign producing a poster with a photograph of refugees at a border crossing, suggesting that 80 million Turks would come to the UK if it stayed in the EU.

The Immigration Act 2014 is the key piece of legislation in the creation of the 'hostile environment'. It introduced a series of requirements on businesses, landlords and public bodies that effectively turned them into immigration officers (Tyler, 2018a). These included:

- a duty on landlords to verify the immigration status of tenants;
- restrictions on migrants opening bank accounts;
- powers to revoke migrants' driving licences;
- further restrictions on access to welfare and benefit services for EU migrants.

At the same time, May introduced a 'deport first, appeal later' policy. This would make it much more difficult for immigrants to win appeals as they would be launching them from outside the UK. These changes were linked to May's hostility to the HRA. At the Conservative Party conference in 2011, May attacked the HRA, claiming that an illegal immigrant avoided deportation because of his pet cat. She was critical of the way that the courts had interpreted article 8 of the HRA – the right to family life – which had been, in May's words, 'perverted'. Foreign national prisoners and illegal immigrants had used the provisions of article 8 to avoid deportation.

Tyler (2018a) notes that there had been an increase in the use of deportation since the early 1990s. The then Home Secretary, John Reed, had pushed for more high-profile media coverage of immigration raids and deportations. In 2010, the Tories had made a pledge to reduce net immigration to the tens of thousands. Such a target could not be met if the UK remained a member of the EU and maintained its commitment to international agreements on asylum and the rights of refugees. In 2012, Capita was given a £40 million contract to find and remove 174,000 migrants who had overstayed on visas that were originally legitimate (Tyler, 2018a). Capita was given access to a Home Office database and sent out a text message stating that the recipient no longer had the right to remain and was required to leave. These actions were about creating a climate of fear; borders are no longer physical, they are also psychological (Back and Sinha, 2018). One of the most notorious aspects of the 'hostile environment' was the so-called Operation Vaken. This pilot took place in July and August 2013 in six London boroughs. Vans were driven round carrying the message 'In the UK illegally? Go home or face arrest'. Alongside these vans, which were driven through some of the most ethnically diverse areas in the country, there was a social media campaign carrying similar messages.

The Windrush scandal

One of the features of the opening ceremony of the 2012 London Olympics was a celebration of the so-called Windrush generation. In June 1948, the Windrush docked at Tilbury, carrying 500 people from Jamaica. These people were citizens of the British Empire and had come to the Mother Country seeking employment. Between 1948 and 1971, approximately 600,000 people from the Caribbean moved to the UK. They played a key role in the development of post-war Britain, for example, it is almost impossible to think of the NHS without highlighting the role that staff from the Caribbean played. Many of those who migrated to the UK travelled as children on their parents' passports but were later to find themselves the victims of the 'hostile environment'. The new requirements placed on employers, landlords and other bodies as result of the Immigration Act 2014 meant that individuals in this group were wrongly classed as illegal immigrants (Gentleman, 2019). Unable to provide the required documentation to show that they were in the country legally, they lost jobs, homes and were denied medical treatment (Gentleman, 2019). Some were even detained and deported to countries in the Caribbean that they had not visited since they had left as children over 50 years earlier.

After the publication of an internal Home Office review into the scandal, Satbir Singh, the Chief Executive of the Joint Council for the Welfare of Immigrants (JCWI), said: 'This review confirms what we at JCWI have said from the beginning: Windrush was no accident, but the inevitable result of a broken immigration system, driven by the divisive politics of scapegoating and scaremongering' (Rawlinson and Gentleman, 2019). At the time of writing, the Home Office is producing a compensation scheme for those affected by the scandal.

Austerity

'Austerity' is a term applied to a series of policies introduced by the Coalition government in the UK. In the aftermath of the banking crisis of 2008, the New Labour government of Gordon Brown followed standard Keynesian policies and bailed out the banks, arguing that they were 'too big to fail'. The estimated cost was £141 billion (Oxfam, 2013). It is often overlooked that as well as the intervention to rescue the banks, Brown introduced a series of other policies to stimulate economic demand, which included a reduction in VAT and increased capital spending. The general election did not produce an overall majority, leading to the Coalition government. While common in European countries, coalition governments are very rare indeed in the UK. Cameron and Clegg argued that the Coalition government was required because of the national fiscal emergency that the country faced as a result of the rise in national debt. The rise was successfully portrayed not as a result of the huge sums used to bail out the banks in 2008, but as a result of profligate spending by the previous Labour government. In responding to the fiscal situation, the Coalition government used a discourse of crisis, emergency and the need for individual sacrifice (Brown, 2015). In tones reminiscent of wartime – the last time there had been a formal coalition – Tory Chancellor of the Exchequer George Osborne claimed that 'we are all in this together'.

The austerity measures that were introduced mark a clear shift from the Keynesian economic policies that the Brown administration had followed from 2008 to 2010. The full impact of austerity was laid bare in the UN rapporteur's report in 2018 (Alston, 2018), which is discussed in more detail in the following. In the 2019 general election campaign, both major parties made public spending commitments that would mark the end of a phase of austerity. It is significant that the major Tory commitments included the recruitment of 20,000 police officers as many commentators pointed out that this would simply reverse the reduction in police numbers that had occurred during the period of austerity.

Austerity was and remains a political project (Krugman, 2015). Following the maxim of 'never letting a serious crisis go to waste', as noted by Mirowski (2013), the election of the Coalition after the banking crisis became an opportunity to complete the recasting of the welfare state. It can be viewed as the final stage of the Thatcherite revolution that commenced in 1979. The aim was for this recasting to be permanent and reduce welfare provision. The policies that underpinned austerity were a very significant break with traditional macroeconomic approaches that would see a fiscal stimulus introduced during an economic downturn (Krugman, 2015). As well as being highly critical of the economics of austerity, Blyth (2013) is also highly critical of the morality of introducing policies that will most affect the poorest to pay for mistakes made by some of the wealthiest in society. Austerity was a targeted policy but the welfare state is a much more complex set of policies than austerity presented it; it does not simply offer protections to the most vulnerable and poorest members of society (Hills, 2017). That said, in the period of austerity, it was those in most need who suffered most. The UK public sector has shrunk to the smallest among major economies (Taylor-Gooby, 2012). The notion of a leaner, smarter and more businesslike state that David Cameron (2015a) proposed involved a significant change in the relationships between individuals, communities and the state. Austerity cannot be understood as purely or solely a matter of economics (Cummins, 2018).

The impact of austerity

Austerity policies were targeted on out-of-work benefits. As noted in Chapter 1, there has been a prolonged and sustained attack on those who are living in poverty, and the discourse of austerity was a further stage in this. Not only were those living in poverty demonised as lazy, workshy and so on, but they were also now responsible for the rise in the national debt. The Coalition government was clear that benefits for pensioners – one of the biggest areas of welfare state spending – would remain untouched. This is an important political constituency, being much more likely to vote and to vote Conservative. In Chapter 1, we saw that the Coalition government was more than willing to use examples such as the Philpott case to push forward its anti-welfare agenda. This agenda is a form of othering as it excludes those in receipt of benefits, particularly out-of-work benefits, from a notion of society. The 'we' in Osborne's 'we are all in this together' is not as inclusive as the phrase seems to imply.

Before the 2015 general election, which returned a Tory majority of 12, the Centre for Welfare Reform (2015) published its *A Fair Society?* report. This report highlighted the following:

- 50 per cent of cuts fall in just two areas that together make up only 25 per cent of government spending;
- the 20 per cent cut in benefits has a disproportionate impact on people with disabilities and people living in poverty;
- there are 40 per cent cuts to local government funding;
- social care funding will be cut by 33 per cent.

The report concluded that:

- people living in poverty bear 39 per cent of all the cuts;
- people with disabilities bear 29 per cent of all the cuts;
- people with severe disabilities bear 15 per cent of all the cuts.

New Labour's policies that had been introduced to tackle child poverty, including Sure Start Centres, Child Trust Funds and targets for reducing child poverty, were immediately sidelined.

The 'bedroom tax' and work capability assessments

The 'bedroom tax' and working capability assessments (WCAs), along with a tougher regime for those claiming benefits, can be seen as emblematic of the austerity regime. WCAs were actually begun under New Labour but the policy was extended under austerity. This also highlights that there are some similarities and continuities between the major parties in these areas and, more broadly, in their attitudes to welfare policy. It is also suggested that both these policies demonstrate the harsher attitudes to welfare that have developed since 1979. Conditionality has always been a feature of the welfare state and benefits system but it has become more deeply engrained in this period. There are some differences in the approaches of both major policies but there are also huge overlaps.

The 'bedroom tax', or, to use its proper title, the 'spare room subsidy', is a change to the Housing Benefit regulations introduced as part of the changes in the Welfare Reform Act 2012. The government argued that the 'bedroom tax' would tackle the situation where tenants were in social housing properties that were too big for their needs. The idea was that the reduced Housing Benefit subsidy would force tenants to move to smaller properties. This was, of course, based on the assumption that such properties were available. Under the 'bedroom tax', Housing Benefit was reduced by 14 per cent if tenants were deemed to have a spare bedroom; the reduction was 25 per cent where tenants have two or more spare rooms. When deciding if a tenant had a spare room, it was assumed that two children aged under 16 of the same gender would be sharing one bedroom. It was also assumed that two children aged under ten, regardless of gender, would be sharing a room. On average, a tenant affected by the bedroom tax lost between £14 and £25 a week and were faced with the choice of making up the shortfall or moving. The government said the move was intended to cut the Housing Benefit bill. In a move that can be seen as setting vulnerable groups against each other, it was claimed that the tax would free up housing to help 300,000 people living in overcrowded accommodation. The DWP set a target of 30 per cent of social housing tenants affected by the changes to move home by 2017. Moffat et al (2015) found that the bedroom tax increased poverty and also had a range of adverse effects on health, well-being and social relationships within this community. Campaigners against the tax also highlighted that these so-called 'spare rooms' were often not spare as they were used for either carers or other vital equipment that disabled family members required.

The WCA system was introduced in 2008 and determines whether an individual is eligible for Employment and Support Allowance. There are three possible outcomes: that the person is fit for work, unfit for work but fit for pre-employment training or fit for neither work nor training. If a person is assessed as being fit for work, then they have to provide detailed evidence of their search for work and applications for jobs. If they fail to comply with these conditions, then they can be sanctioned, that is, benefits will be stopped for a period of between four and 78 weeks (18 months). A claimant could be sanctioned, for example, if they lost an employment scheme place through misconduct or without good reason, or did not go to meetings on time with their adviser or work coach, or take part in interviews. The DWP presents the WCA as a way of getting people 'off benefits and into work'. In another example of the shifting nature of the welfare state and increased private involvement, the original contract was won by Atos. It was then taken over by Maximus, another private company.

There have been huge concerns about the operation and impact of the WCA process. The WCA is essentially a functionality test. This makes it difficult to convey the complexity and impact of a range of potential health and disability conditions. For example, mental health conditions will fluctuate and they may not physically prevent an individual from working, but mean that it is impossible for them to carry out their normal role. People with mental health issues and disabilities face well-documented stigma in the workplace and job market. It is important that they are offered appropriate support and advice. However, the WCA has been seen as essentially punitive, with its main aim being to reduce public expenditure.

Barr et al's (2016) analysis is the first study of the impact of the introduction of the WCA process. The study found that the WCA was associated with:

- 590 suicides;
- 725,000 additional prescriptions for antidepressants;
- 279,000 additional cases of self-reported mental health problems.

Putting these figures into context, the authors state that they represent:

- 5 per cent of the total number of suicides;
- 5 per cent of the total number of antidepressant prescriptions;
- 11 per cent of self-reported mental health problems.

Barr et al (2016) conclude that the negative impact of this kind of welfare reform outweighs any potential benefit as it is likely to lead to increased expenditure in other areas. The authors conclude that although the explicit aim of welfare reform in the UK is to reduce 'dependency', it is likely that targeting people living in the most vulnerable conditions with policies that are harmful to health will have the opposite effect.

There have been a number of significant shifts in the nature of poverty since 1979. One has been generational: changes to pensions, the extension of homeownership and the rise in the value of property have combined to mean that older people are less likely to be living in poverty than used to be the case. The government's so-called 'triple lock' on pensions meant that they were unaffected by austerity. The triple lock guaranteed that the basic state pension will rise by a minimum of 2.5 per cent, the rate of inflation or average earnings growth, whichever is greater. Before 2011, the state pension rose in line with the retail prices index (RPI) measure of inflation, which has been consistently lower than annual rises in earnings or 2.5 per cent. The second change has been the rise of in-work poverty. The Conservative and Labour Parties have consistently presented employment as being the most effective means of combating poverty. However, the majority of those living in poverty are actually in work (Joseph Rowntree Foundation, 2016), which is the result of the development of the gig economy and zero-hours contracts, combined with the 1 per cent cap on public sector pay. Furthermore, the impact of austerity has been racialised and gendered (Emejulu and Bassel,

2015): as the public sector employs more women than other sectors of the economy, wage stagnation in this area impacts disproportionately on women.

The most vulnerable individuals and groups in society are those who have greatest need of and are most likely to use public services. They are also most likely to be subject to the punitive aspects of welfare regimes. The policies of austerity will have most impact on the poorest, including families with children (Crossley, 2016). It is these groups that have paid the greatest price for austerity (Beatty and Fothergill, 2016), especially as local authorities in the poorest areas with the highest needs have faced the biggest cuts (Crossley, 2016).

UN rapporteur: poverty in the UK

The UN special rapporteur on extreme poverty and human rights, Philip Alston, visited the UK in November 2018. Alston's role is to report to the UN Human Rights Council. The special rapporteur has to outline if government policies and programmes relating to extreme poverty are consistent with its human rights obligations. The special rapporteur can then make recommendations to the government and other stakeholders. The special rapporteur received over 300 written submissions and held consultations across the country. His final report was a damning indictment of the impact of austerity policies, concluding that the welfare state that had been established after the Second World War had been shredded (Alston, 2018). The report was emphatic that austerity was an ideological and political project. It noted that the policy was a failure on its own terms as it had failed to reduce government debt, which had grown significantly since 2010. While highlighting the devastating impact of austerity, Alston (2018) also made clear that he had witnessed tremendous resilience in the face of adversity.

The final report begins by placing the UK in a broader context. Despite the economic difficulties that it faces, the UK is the world's fifth-largest economy, a leading centre of global finance and has the fundamentals of a strong economy (Alston, 2018). At the time of Alston's visit, unemployment was at a record low. Despite this economic prosperity, Alston (2018) outlines the impact of the changes to the welfare system, with poverty among children and pensioners on the rise. The following highlights the extent and nature of poverty in the UK:

- 14 million people live in poverty;
- 4 million of those are more than 50 per cent below the poverty line;
- 1.5 million experienced destitution in 2017;
- relative child poverty rates are expected to increase by 7 per cent between 2015 and 2021;
- child poverty rates will reach nearly 40 per cent by 2021.

Alston (2018: 3) concludes that 'For almost one in every two children to be poor in twenty-first century Britain would not just be a disgrace, but a social calamity and an economic disaster rolled into one.'

Behind these damning statistics are the everyday stories of people whose lives have been turned upside down. Alston (2018) notes that despite a series of official denials, the damage to the social fabric is apparent. There has been a steep rise in the number of people using food banks, which did not exist in the UK before the introduction of austerity. In fact, food banks have been a key feature of the welfare landscape (Garthwaite, 2016). Tory ministers have had two broad responses to the increase in the use of food banks. The first is to blame those who use food banks for being unable to manage their finances, which is a modern play on long-standing tropes that portray those living in poverty as inadequate (Welshman, 2013; Wintour, 2013). In fact, benefit sanctions are one of the major drivers of food-bank use. The second response is to praise the volunteers who run food banks as an example of British community spirit and the values of the Big Society. The report also highlights major increases in homelessness and rough sleeping. Alongside these developments, the Legal Aid budget has been slashed, making it much more difficult for the government to be held to account.

Alston (2018) concludes that the broader social safety net that provided at least some form of minimal protection has been removed. Austerity has had a particularly devastating impact on local authority funding. The impact of these cuts can be seen in the reduction in social services, the closure of local libraries, reduced police numbers and the collapse of many youth and community services. It is important to emphasise here that these impacts are disproportionately felt by the poorest in communities, who are the most reliant on public services. Alston (2018) notes that the result is a level of social dislocation that resulted in the government appointing a Minister for Suicide Prevention. Alston's (2018: 4) overall conclusion is a stark one: 'The bottom line is that much of the glue that has held British society together since the Second World War has been deliberately removed and replaced with a harsh and uncaring ethos.'

Welfare reforms

The special rapporteur's report discusses the impact of welfare reforms. It concludes that benefit changes since 2010 have saved money but have made it more difficult for people to escape poverty. The report praises the 'triple lock' on pensions because of its impact in reducing pensioner poverty. However, the 'triple lock' is contrasted with the freeze on benefits rates for those of working age. The nature of poverty means that those living in poorer households have to spend more of the family income on basic consumer goods and necessities. The government froze benefit rates in 2016; thus, inflation, even at its relatively low level, reduces the value of benefits. Poor families have had to do more with less as the price of goods has gone up and the value of their income has declined. Households are expected to cope with a reduction of £4.4 billion in 2019–20 alone. Housing Benefit has been decimated amid a real crisis in affordable housing. Other changes, such as the cap on benefits for working-age households and limiting benefits to two children per family, have combined to increase the pressures on those living in poverty.

One of the most disturbing aspects of austerity has been the reduction in the Legal Aid budget – described as a decimation by Alston. The Legal Aid, Sentencing and Punishment of Offenders Act 2012 (LASPO) excluded most housing, benefits and family law cases from Legal Aid. The changes in Legal Aid mean that those without resources find it increasingly difficult, if not impossible, to challenge the decisions of public bodies. Public law in areas such as housing and family law is increasingly complex. It also includes vitally important areas such as child custody cases. An investigation by *The Guardian* revealed that the cuts meant that parents were unable to challenge decisions where their children had been taken into public care (Bowcott et al, 2018). The investigation revealed the extent of the impact of legal cuts:

- an increase in unrepresented litigants in family courts, which prevented many from continuing the case;
- an 88 per cent fall in the number of people accessing Legal Aid in family matters;
- more victims of domestic violence being cross-examined by ex-partners;
- hundreds of thousands of people not being able to pursue cases in other areas, such as housing, debt, employment, clinical negligence, immigration, welfare payments and education.

These changes represent a huge shift in the balance between individuals, families and the state – a shift that has been rather hidden.

Universal Credit

UC has become the symbol of both austerity and the welfare reforms that the Coalition government introduced. The UN rapporteur's report notes that at its conception and introduction, UC represented a potentially significant streamlining of the incredibly complex benefit system. However, the rolling out of the programme has been far removed from this ideal. Alston (2018: 4) suggests that UC is 'fast falling into Universal Discredit'.

The aim of UC was to consolidate six different benefits into one. As Alston (2018) states, the aim of social welfare should be to provide routes out of poverty and an efficient streamlined system will play a key role in this. However, the design and rollout of UC was 'more concerned with making economic savings and sending messages about lifestyles than responding to the multiple needs of those living with a disability, job loss, housing insecurity, illness, and the demands of parenting' (Alston, 2018: 5). The overall impact has been negative, with Alston (2018) noting that the negative impacts have not just been financial, but also included detrimental effects on claimants' mental health. Alston (2018: 5) angrily describes the government's response as 'almost entirely dismissive, blaming political opponents for wanting to sabotage their work, or suggesting that the media didn't really understand the system and that Universal Credit was unfairly blamed for problems rooted in the old legacy system of benefits'. UC has an inbuilt difficulty: the five-week payment delay. When someone successfully claims UC, they have to wait at least five weeks for a payment. This 'waiting period' is often much longer and can take up to 12 weeks. The delay means that those who may already be in crisis are forced into debt, rent arrears and serious hardship. The majority of claimants seek 'advance payments', which, in turn, must be repaid to the DWP. Debts to the DWP and to third parties can be deducted from UC at a higher rate than under previous benefit rules. Alston (2018) is unequivocal and states that the UC rules are based on wanting to send a clear message that claiming and living on benefits should involve hardship. The UC system does this by immediately ensuring that claimants are in debt. The vast majority of the working population would struggle if they were denied wages for a period of five to 12 weeks.

The process of claiming and demonstrating that you are looking for work is felt to be demeaning, and claimants are being forced into precarious, poorly paid work. UC involves the imposition of sanctions resulting in the loss of benefit for a range of infringements, many of which seem relatively minor. Alston (2018) records that he was presented with a great deal of anecdotal evidence that demonstrated the harsh and arbitrary nature of some of the sanctions. The inquiry undertaken by the UN Committee on the Rights of Persons with Disabilities found 'evidence of grave and systematic violation of the rights of persons with disabilities', partly on the basis of the sanctions regime (United Nations CRPD, 2017). Dwyer et al (2019) demonstrate not only the harsh reality of the sanctions regime, but also that it is, even on its own terms, largely ineffectual.

Alongside the fundamental difficulties with the structure of UC, it was introduced at a time when the 2017 Government Transformation Strategy meant that government services will become 'digital by default'. This has had huge implications for the benefits system. Alston (2018) argues that a digital welfare state is emerging that will have huge impacts on the human rights of the most vulnerable in the UK. UC was the first benefit to be 'digital by default'. This means that all claims and inquiries are made online and that claimants interact with authorities mainly through an online portal. However, there is a fundamental weakness and injustice here as the group most likely to claim UC is made up of the most vulnerable, who are also more likely to have poor digital literacy and/or Internet access. Alston (2018) notes that the expansion of Internet usage for many daily tasks such as shopping and banking obscures the fact that there are many groups who do not feel confident in these areas. He concludes that 'Universal Credit has built a digital barrier that effectively obstructs many individuals' access to their entitlements. Women, older people, people who do not speak English and the disabled are more likely to be unable to overcome this hurdle' (Alston, 2018: 6).

Community and other groups are struggling to support the numbers of people who need assistance. Alston (2018) highlights the fact that public libraries, which have faced significant budget cuts, have had to cope with large numbers of UC claimants. In Newcastle, the first city where 'full service' UC was rolled out in May 2016, the City Library digitally assisted nearly 2,000 customers between August 2017 and September 2018.

Austerity: the impact on people living with disabilities

Frances Ryan's (2019) book *Crippled: Austerity and the Demonization of Disabled People* outlines the impact of austerity and welfare reform on people living with disabilities. As noted earlier, welfare reforms such as the 'bedroom tax' and the benefit cap had a disproportionate impact on people living with disabilities. In her book, Ryan draws a contrast between the coverage of the 2012 Paralympics, where Cameron portrayed the UK as a trailblazer, and the reality of welfare retrenchment, which targeted people living with disabilities. The abolition of the Disability Living Allowance and its replacement with Personal Independence Payments, alongside fitness-to-work tests and the broader cuts in social care, all had a greater impact on people living with disabilities. This group of people already face a number of barriers to entry into the labour market and are therefore more likely to be in receipt of benefits of one kind or another. Changes in these systems have huge impacts but these are often hidden from the wider public. Ryan (2019) argues that these current policies cannot be divorced from the historical policies of institutionalisation and the denial of civil rights to people living with disabilities. The impact of austerity also demonstrates that hard-won civil rights can be rolled back very quickly.

Alston (2018) does not gild his conclusions in polite diplomatic language; rather, he states categorically that austerity and the poverty it created was a political choice. In 2017, the Treasury decided to use available resources to fund tax cuts rather than tackle some of the impacts of austerity outlined in his report. He quotes Hobbes (2016), who claimed that without a social contract, life outside society would be 'solitary, poor, nasty, brutish, and short'. The public institutions that formed the social contract and brought communities together have been dismantled or undermined. Alston's (2018: 22) bleak conclusion is that the 'next generation's prospects are already being grievously undermined by the systematic dismantling of social protection policies since 2010'.

Conclusion

David Cameron's premiership will inevitably be viewed through the prism of Brexit and its aftermath. Having set out to settle the internal divisions in the Tory Party once and for all, he ended up resigning. Cameron is often portrayed by his critics within the Tory Party as a metropolitan social liberal – part of the 'Notting Hill set' – and somewhat divorced from the average Tory voter. Apart from his views on gay marriage, there is actually little evidence from his social policy agenda of this. Far from being socially liberal and economically conservative, he was conservative in both areas. Austerity was a recasting of the welfare state that inflicted huge damage on individuals, families and communities. It was also a policy that targeted the most vulnerable, which is something that a true social liberal would surely avoid. The politics of austerity saw the Coalition government using the cover of the financial crisis to undertake a fundamental retrenchment of the welfare state. The Big Society should not be dismissed as a political gimmick or rhetoric; rather, it reflects an aspiration for a recasting of the relationship between citizens and the social state. This recasting is presented as a fiscal necessity but is actually driven by a politics that is underpinned by the othering of the poor. Despite Cameron's and the Coalition's claims to social liberalism, they followed a series of policies that shredded the social state.

8

Conclusion: Citizenship and the Centaur State

Introduction

Despite differences in tone and texture between political parties and administrations since 1979, there has been a clear rightwards shift in welfare and penal policy. These trends have led to the creation of what Wacquant (2012, 2016) has termed a 'centaur state'. The dual nature of the 'centaur state' sees an increase in personal freedoms for the elites in society and the deregulation of the market, while, in a counterpoint to these processes, the punitive turn in welfare and penal policy sees the state taking harsher positions in approaches to disciplining poorer members of society. Wacquant (2008, 2009a, 2009b) has termed these shifts in welfare and penal policy 'prisonfare', that is, a combination of workfare and prison. These changes have profound implications for the exercise of citizenship (Somers, 2008). These shifts have been intensified by the period of austerity. The cumulative effect of austerity policies can be seen in the underfunding of public services and a reduction in the incomes of the poorest members of society. The poorest members of society have paid for the errors of some of the wealthiest (Blyth, 2013) The UN rapporteur's report (Alston, 2018) laid out in clear detail the social and economic damage that these policies created. The most damaging cuts were experienced in the poorest areas (Crossley, 2016), which are the areas that were most hit by the previous policies of deindustrialisation and moves towards a service-based economy. Bourdieu (1999) concluded that the poorest areas of our cities have become characterised by 'absence', that is, they have been abandoned by the welfare-oriented institutions of the state.

Neoliberalism as market fundamentalism

Somers (2008) regards neoliberalism as a form of 'market fundamentalism'. This captures not only the zeal of true believers, but also the way that the key ideas moved from the margins to the mainstream in the mid-1970s. Like a religion, there were a series of key texts as well as high priests who spread the true beliefs. These can be reduced to a core belief in not only the moral and economic superiority of the market, but also the need for its principles to be applied to all areas of social life. This belief in the market is combined with a deep-rooted anti-statism. This market fundamentalism is a modern form of what Polanyi (1957) termed a 'stark utopia', that is, a world dominated by a self-regulating market economy. Somers and Block (2005) argue that the fundamentalist nature of neoliberalism sets it apart from other forms of market-oriented economics that allow for and recognise the need for a role for the state (Chang, 2010). As with other forms of fundamentalist belief, there is a gap between the pure philosophical model and the actuality of policies pursued by states in real-world market economies. Market fundamentalism, or neoliberalism, has become the dominant spirit of the age. As we have seen, its influence is not limited to the economic sphere, but extends to the wider culture.

One of the key tenets of market fundamentalism is the notion that the welfare state is wasteful, is open to exploitation and fraud, creates dependency, and achieves the reverse of what it sets out to do. These claims can be traced back to Malthus (1985 [1798]). Malthus's attack on the Poor Laws argued that they created a series of perverse incentives. He claimed that the new parish family allowances meant that poorer families had more children than they could afford and the burden of caring for these children was transferred to the state. Malthus went on to argue that this new system was morally corrupting as it meant that the poor were no longer independent or reliant on their own resources. Malthus saw this corruption leading to a decline in sexual morality and wider civic behaviour. These themes have been found in right-wing criticisms of welfare ever since (Welshman, 2013). From Malthus to Murray and beyond, the root of the problems in these models is always individual behaviour: the poor are poor because of the individual choices that they make. Hirschmann (1991) outlined the way that historical critics of welfare have used the 'rhetoric of perversity' to argue that the welfare state, by creating dependency, makes the lives of the poor worse. The logic of this position is that, to use a modern phrase, 'tough love' is required. These views can be seen in the moves towards a more punitive approach to welfare. The system places more demands on claimants and introduces more demeaning administrative processes (Flint, 2019).

One of the key questions to ask is: how did market fundamentalism move from the margins to the mainstream? The establishment of the post-Second World War welfare state in Britain saw the dominance of Keynesian approaches to the management of the economy. These were based on a government commitment to full employment, a recognition of the role for government in the management of demand and the establishment and investment in public services (Kynaston, 2008, 2010, 2014). The price paid for the austerity that followed the Second World War was the establishment of the welfare state (Todd, 2014). The contrast with the austerity of the Coalition years, which saw the shredding of that social contract, could hardly be greater. The impact of the oil crisis in the early 1970s provided the opportunity that led to changes in policy and the resurgence of the New Right. As noted in Chapter 2, Thatcher in the UK and Reagan in the US exploited the political and economic crises of the late 1970s to argue very effectively that governments were the cause of, not the solution to, these problems. In terms of the welfare state, there was a development of a new form of 'poverty knowledge' (O'Connor, 2001). This new knowledge was essentially a modernised version of the long-standing attacks on the welfare state. However, these ideas were quickly spread via a network of academics (for example, Murray, 1990; Mead, 1991), think tanks and sympathetic journalists. These rhetorical shifts led to anti-welfarism becoming reinvigorated and moving into the mainstream. Giroux (2011) noted that one of the cultural impacts of the dominance of neoliberal ideas was the crowding out of more socially oriented ideas. Beckett and Western (2001) argue that wider social policy is inextricably linked with developments in penal policy. In their analysis, political cultures that emphasise the social causes of marginality and offending are much more likely to have a penal policy based on integration. The welfare and penal systems cannot be divorced from each other; both have become more punitive.

One of the key tenets of neoliberalism is that the so-called efficiency and discipline of the market can and should be applied to all areas of provision. Since 1979, there has been an increase in the so-called marketisation of the state, which is particularly the case in the areas of welfare and penal policy. This period has seen private companies running prisons and supervising offenders, as well as managing contracts such as the WCA process. In addition to concerns about the way that companies profit from these contracts, this privatisation process raises fundamental ethical questions about the role of the state. Market fundamentalism acknowledges that the state has a role in maintaining law and order; in fact, this is its key role (Nozick, 1974). However, this does not mean that these functions cannot be exercised by private contractors. Those opposed to this position argue, for example, that it is wrong to profit from the incarceration of individuals. In addition, the excesses of the market can be seen in the exploitation of a number of these contracts, for example, G4S has been fined over £7 million since 2010 for breaches of contract and poor service provision, and was also given a lucrative £25 million contract to manage the electronic tagging of offenders despite a Serious Fraud Office investigation into its practices. It is not just commercial companies that have been privileged in these new models of service provision; the government has been much more supportive of charities and the third sector, though large charities operate much more as commercial enterprises. Cameron's notion of the Big Society can be seen as the ultimate outcome of this anti-statism and suspicion of local authority welfare professionals. Kids Company was founded in 1996 by Camila Batmanghelidjh, a prominent public figure who appeared to have the ear of both the Blair and Cameroon governments. The Select Affairs Committee's inquiry into the collapse of Kids Company noted that despite concerns being raised about the organisation, successive governments provided Kids Company with grants of at least £42 million. This is in addition to the celebrity support and donations that the organisation was able to receive.

Advanced marginality

There is no real doubt that neoliberalism, albeit in several variants, has assumed a dominant political and economic position since 1979. As we have seen, following the fall of the Soviet Union, some (for example, Fukuyama, 1992) argued that this was the inevitable and desirable outcome of political history. There were and are pockets of resistance to the neoliberal project but these have not been able to survive its forward march. Nearly two decades later, even Fukuyama (2018) himself accepts that history has not ended and there are new forms of political, social and economic debate. The climate crisis, the crisis in social care and the unravelling of the political process and institutions are all challenges that will not be solved by the application of market disciplines; rather, they are, in fact, the product of them (Somers, 2008; Brown, 2015, 2019; Fraser, 2017b).

The impact of neoliberal economic and social policies is clear, including not only an increase in inequality and poverty, but also a rhetorical shift. Murray's (1990) 'underclass' discourse has been largely uncritically accepted across the major political parties – certainly in the US and the UK. This discourse has a strong eugenicist underpinning (Slater, 2014). In the UK, these changes manifest themselves most clearly in popular culture and tabloid media, where the demonisation of the poor is widespread (Tyler, 2008; Shildrick et al, 2009; Jensen, 2014). The term 'advanced marginality' is used to capture the impact of these economic, social and cultural changes. Inequality is not simply a matter of economic resources, though this is a fundamentally important area; it also has social, physical and psychological impacts (Wilkinson and Pickett, 2009). Poverty has become spatial concentrated. We saw earlier how the term 'sink estate' has entered the political and popular discourse, carrying with it a series of stigmatising notions. Wacquant (2010) argues that the underclass discourse not only corrodes the sense of self of residents, but also makes it more difficult to develop and maintain broader social relationships. Stigmatisation is a function entwined with social, economic and political power and capital (Tyler, 2018b). The labelling of individuals and the construction of stereotypes is the product of processes of disapproval, rejection and discrimination.

Wacquant (2016) argues that these new forms of increasingly spatially concentrated forms of poverty have been combined with new forms of social regulations. These relationships include increasingly punitive policies that are applied in a whole range of areas, for example, social housing tenants have to sign up to good behaviour contracts and welfare claimants are subject to a regime that imposes conditions (Flint, 2019). These combine with the expansion of the penal state to produce new disciplinary mechanisms – a form of 'authoritarian therapeutism' (Wacquant, 2013: 249).

The aim of these processes is not only to 'correct' behaviour, but also to link people to the precarious job market, where workers have been stripped of rights and protections (Standing, 2011). The increased use of welfare conditionality is part of the wider processes outlined earlier that seek to present poverty and the solutions to it as individual issues. These policies are heavily influenced by those such as Murray (1990) and Mead (1992), who see the problems of poverty not as an outcome of the market, but as the result of individual failings. In addition, the work of both Murray and Mead has racist and eugenicist undercurrents.

Flint (2019) carried out important research that sought to explore the impact of these processes of conditionality. The research looked at these issues from the perspectives of not only those subject to the processes, but also the officials who were faced with the challenges of enacting policies defined by central government. One of the enduring strengths of Lipsky's (1980) concept of street-level bureaucracy is the way that it highlights the often contradictory positions in which welfare officials, social workers and police officers are often placed. Street-level bureaucrats exercise authority as well as autonomy, and they often have to enact policy that they do not support or that runs counter to their professional values. This is a complex area. Flint (2019) shows how practitioners interviewed often articulated views about inadequate parenting, joblessness and lack of engagement in education that echoed the official 'underclass'-influenced discourse. However, there were also examples in the housing sector where officials were troubled by their role in the implementation of policies that led to the eviction of children and families, such as good behaviour contracts. These officials also highlighted the fact that one of the (unintended) consequences of these systems is that people become more difficult to engage and may even disappear from official sight, which makes people vulnerable to wider exploitation. Another important finding from this research was a challenge to the policy discourse of welfare dependency as most of the participants were committed to work. This was coupled with the view that they were most likely to find low-paid precarious work, which echoes Shildrick and MacDonald's (2012) findings about the precarious labour market. This research highlights the complexity of the negotiations between individuals within modern welfare bureaucracies as these bureaucracies are, in Bourdieu's (2001) terms, 'shotted through with the contradictions of the state'. However, the direction of travel is clear: the state has moved further towards the disciplinary pole.

The centaur state

Fraser outlined her notion of 'progressive neoliberalism' as a way of describing the dominant political discourse from the 1990s onwards, which is a combination of ideas that are, on the surface, socially progressive and neoliberal economics. There is a paradox of more liberal social attitudes and policies in areas of race, gender and sexuality being espoused by those committed to market economics that entrenches marginalisation, discrimination and stigma. She sums this combination up as follows:

> Drawing on progressive forces from civil society, they diffused a recognition ethos that was superficially egalitarian and emancipatory. At the core of this ethos were ideals of 'diversity,' women's 'empowerment,' and LGBTQ

[lesbian, gay, bisexual, trans and queer] rights; post-racialism, multiculturalism, and environmentalism. These ideals were interpreted in a specific, limited way that was fully compatible with the Goldman Sachsification of the U.S. economy. Protecting the environment meant carbon trading. Promoting home ownership meant subprime loans bundled together and resold as mortgage-backed securities. Equality meant meritocracy. (Fraser, 2017a)

Fraser is clearly not arguing against progressive, feminist and anti-racist ideas and politics; rather, she is arguing against the way that neoliberalism has used the ideas that are rooted in radical social movements. An example of this would be Sandberg's (2013) *Lean In*, written by the Chief Operating Officer of Facebook. This is a guide to corporate success written by a billionaire and packaged as a feminist tract. Fraser sees the era of Trump and post-Brexit Britain as signalling the end of the era of progressive neoliberalism.

Neoliberalism and citizenship

The changes that have been outlined in this volume have had a profound impact on the nature of citizenship and the relationship between individuals, communities and the state. At the heart of neoliberal political philosophy is a suspicion of the state because it sees a potential for the state to restrict individual freedom and choice. Citizenship becomes contractualised and a form of exchange, and previous notions of citizenship based on the recognition of political, economic, social and cultural rights have been undermined. Neoliberalism produces a form of atomising, hyper-individualism. Giroux sums up the impact of neoliberalism as follows: 'In the midst of a massive global attack on the welfare state and social provisions fueled by neoliberal policies, the social contract central to liberal democracies has been shredded and with it any viable notion of solidarity, economic justice and the common good' (Giroux, 2017). At the heart of the development of neoliberal social policy is the notion of individualism, which means that there is a suspicion of state bureaucracies and bureaucrats. The shifts that have been outlined in this volume have removed the state from areas of welfare provision. The focus on individualism has positive aspects, as in its commitment to personal freedom; however, as Brown (2015: 132) notes, it also has the affect of individualising problems and responsibility for them. This means that the responsibility for structural issues such as unemployment and environmental problems are 'sent down the pipeline to small and weak units unable to cope with them technically, politically or financially' (Brown, 2010). Brown concludes that this devolution process results in a situation where these smaller units are given decision-making authority but lack the resources to enact policies.

Somers (2008) outlines three key elements in society: the state, the market and civil society. In the advance of neoliberalism, the application of market mechanisms means that the notion of the social or social goods is squeezed out. This means that the overall impacts of policies that result in economic and social inequality are not fully considered. Neoliberalism is dynamic but the constant creation of winners and losers ignores wider social damages, such as financial speculation and environmental damage. Wacquant (2008, 2009a, 2009b) outlines the fact that neoliberal policies have attacked not only the formal social state, but also the institutions of civil society. In Somers's (2008) model of society, the institutions of civil society – trade unions, social movements, community groups and so on – act as a counterbalance to both the market and the state.

Somers (2008) argues that neoliberalism has a deeply corrosive impact on citizenship. It is important that we do not construct citizenship solely in terms of formal legal rights as it is important that individuals also have a meaningful role in society. This would include not only political representation, but also the means for translating them into substantive rights in practice. For Somers, the way that the state abandoned poor African-Americans in the wake of Hurricane Katrina is a prime example of the logical outcome of these processes, whereby not all citizens are regarded as moral equals. She argues that the victims of Hurricane Katrina were, in effect, internally stateless persons (Somers, 2008: 118). The result of market fundamentalism is that many people and groups have lost active membership of civil society.

Somers (2008), in her discussion of modern citizenship, uses a term borrowed from Arendt (2017): the 'right to rights'. The existence of de jure rights does not mean that citizens can de facto enjoy them. All three elements – the state, the market and civil society – have to be in balance and functioning to create meaningful political citizenship. The state has a key role in limiting the potential excesses of the most powerful actors in the market and civil society. Civil society does not, in and of itself, have the resources and power to challenge the market. Somers (2008) concludes that in the absence of a robust state infrastructure, civil society leads to a form of conservative communitarianism.

Conclusion: from the war on poverty to the war on the poor

The term 'centaur state' is most closely associated with the work of Wacquant (2008, 2009a, 2009b). Wacquant strongly argues that the expansion of the penal state is an endogenous feature of the neoliberal project. For Wacquant (2009b: 4), neoliberalism is a class project that has produced a new form of statecraft characterised by the 'amputation of its economic arm, the retraction of its social bosom, and the massive expansion of its penal fist'. The result is a form of 'double regulation': the reduction of the social state and the expansion of the prison system. Wacquant (2009a) notes that as these processes directed at the poor were developing, there was a parallel process of liberalising attitudes towards the elites and corporations. While Wacquant's (2009a, 2009b) work is focused on the US, he argues that the 'centaur state' is a global phenomenon, though taking specifically local and national forms. The penal state is stronger and the welfare state weaker in the US because of a range of historical factors, including the history of slavery and racism, the cultural importance of individualism, and the comparative weakness of organised labour. Neoliberalism involves the 'rolling back' of the welfare state but 'rolling out' of the penal/disciplinary state.

Wacquant (2009a, 2009b) is wary of models that fails to recognise that the state is far from monolithic. He uses Bourdieu's notion of the 'bureaucratic field' to examine the debates and struggles within state structures. He sees that there are separate axes to these struggles: one is the struggle between the higher state actors who promote neoliberalism and the street-level bureaucrats (Lipsky, 1980) who enact policies on a day-to-day basis; the other is between the left hand of the state – the social state – and the right hand of the state – the punitive state. Within these processes, the othering and stigmatising portrayal of the poor has an important function. Wacquant (2009a, 2009b) concludes that the modern penal state has developed a key role in the production and management of inequality and this represents a fundamental shift. Piven and Cloward (2012: xiii) argued that the welfare state goes through cyclical changes in responses to political and economic pressure:

> Historical evidence suggests that relief arrangements are initiated or expanded during the occasional outbreaks of civil disorder produced by mass unemployment, and are then abolished or contracted when political stability is

restored. We shall argue that expansive relief policies are designed to mute civil disorder, and restrictive ones to reinforce work norms.

Wacquant argues that this thesis no longer holds and the penal state has replaced the welfare state as the means of regulating the poor. Thus, for Wacquant (2009a, 2009b), the penal state is not a reaction to increasing crime rates; it is a reaction to social insecurity.

The modern notion of the 'centaur state' is represented by Wacquant (2009a, 2009b) as a new form of the management of marginality. However, the period since 1979 is not the only one where an economic crisis has led to the double regulation of the poor. Hobsbawm (1994) outlines that in the interwar period in the UK, there was a rise in the prison population and the introduction of a very brutal form of workfare, which saw the establishment of a series of labour camps. Conditionality, in some form or another, has always been a feature of welfare regimes. Prisoners have always been much more likely to come from marginalised social backgrounds and groups. While recognising these historical continuities, it is also important to recognise that there is something about the nature and degree of these processes of marginalisation which mean that the post-1979 period marks a clear rupture from the social-democratic Keynesian regimes that went before.

References

Adler, M. and Longhurst, B. (2002) *Discourse Power and Justice*. Abingdon: Routledge.

Akers, R. and Sellers, C. (2008) *Criminological Theories: Introduction, Evaluation, and Application* (5th edn). New York, NY: Oxford University Press USA.

Alexander, M. (2012) *The New Jim Crow: Mass Incarceration in the Age of Colorblindness*. New York, NY: New Press.

Alston, P. (2018) 'Statement on visit to the United Kingdom, by Professor Philip Alston, United Nations special rapporteur on extreme poverty and human rights', www.ohchr.org/Documents/Issues/Poverty/EOM_GB_16Nov2018.pdf

Arendt, H. (2017) *The Origins of Totalitarianism*. London: Penguin.

Babiak, P., Hare, R.D. and McLaren, T. (2006) *Snakes in Suits: When Psychopaths Go to Work*. New York, NY: Regan Books.

Back, L. and Sinha, S. (2018) *Migrant City*. Abingdon: Routledge.

Baldwin, B. (2018) 'Black, white, and blue: bias, profiling, and policing in the age of Black Lives Matter', *New England Law Review*, 40: 431.

Barr, B., Taylor-Robinson, D., Stuckler, D., Loopstra, R., Reeves, A., Wickham, S. and Whitehead, M. (2016) 'Fit-for-work or fit-for-unemployment? Does the reassessment of disability benefit claimants using a tougher work capability assessment help people into work?', *Journal Epidemiology and Community Health*, 70(5): 452–8.

Bauman, Z. (1989) *Modernity and the Holocaust*. Cambridge: Polity Press.

Bauman, Z. (1991) *Modernity and Ambivalence*. Cambridge: Polity Press.

Bauman, Z. (2007) *Liquid Modernity. Living in an Age of Uncertainty*. Cambridge: Polity Press.

Bauman, Z. (2008) *The Art of Life*. Cambridge: Polity Press.

Bauman, Z. (2011) 'The London riots 2011: on consumerism coming home to roost', *Social Europe Journal,* 9, https://dedona.wordpress.com/2011/08/11/the-london-riots-%E2%80%93-on-consumerism-coming-home-to-roost-zygmunt-bauman/

BBC (2011) 'England riots: "The whites have become black" says David Starkey', www.bbc.co.uk/news/av/uk-14513517

Beatty, C. and Fothergill, S. (2016) *The Uneven Impact of Welfare Reform: The Financial Losses to Places and People*. Sheffield: Sheffield Hallam University.

Beck, U. (1992) *Risk Society: Towards a New Modernity*. London: Sage.

Becker, G.S. (1968) 'Crime and punishment: an economic approach', *Journal of Political Economy*, 76: 169–217.

Beckett, K. and Western, B. (2001) 'Governing social marginality: Welfare, incarceration, and the transformation of state policy', *Punishment & Society*, 3(1): 43–59.

Bellamy, R. (1991) *Hayek and Modern Liberalism*. Oxford: Clarendon Press.

Benyon, J. (2012) 'England's urban disorder: the 2011 riots', *Political Insight*, 3(1): 12–17.

Berlin, I.N. (2002 [1958]) 'Two concepts of liberty', in H. Hardy (ed) *Liberty*. Oxford: Oxford University Press, pp 166–217.

Blackmon, D. (2008) *Slavery by Another Name: The Re-enslavement of Black Americans from the Civil War to World War II*. New York, NY: Anchor Books.

Blair, T. (2010) *My Political Life: A Journey*. New York, NY: Knopf.

Blyth, M. (2013) *Austerity: The History of a Dangerous Idea*. Oxford: Oxford University Press.

Boltanski, L. and Chiapello, E. (2005) 'The new spirit of capitalism', *International Journal of Politics, Culture, and Society*, 18(3/4): 161–88.

Borrie, G. (1994) 'Social justice: strategies for national renewal', www.ippr.org/files/publications/pdf/commission-on-social-justice_final_2014.pdf

Bourdieu, P. (1999) *The Weight of the World: Social Suffering in Contemporary Society*. Cambridge: Polity Press.

Bourdieu, P. (2001) *Acts of Resistance: Against the New Myths of Our Time*. Cambridge: Polity Press.

Bowcott, O., Hill, A. and Duncan, P. (2018) 'Revealed: legal aid cuts forcing parents to give up fight for children', *Guardian*, 26 December, www.theguardian.com/law/2018/dec/26/revealed-legal-aid-cuts-forcing-parents-to-give-up-fight-for-children

Bridges, L. (2013) 'The case against joint enterprise', *Race & Class*, 54(4): 33–42.

Brough, P., Chataway, S. and Briggs, A. (2016) '"You don't want people knowing you're a copper!" A contemporary assessment of police organisational culture', *International Journal of Police Science & Management*, 18(1): 28–36.

Brown, G. (1999) 'Equality – then and now', in D. Leonard (ed) *Crosland and New Labour*. Basingstoke: Macmillan.

Brown, L.K. (2004) 'Officer or overseer: why police desegregation fails as an adequate solution to racist, oppressive, and violent policing in black communities', *New York University Review of Law and Social Change*, 29: 757.

Brown, W. (2015) *Undoing the Demos: Neoliberalism's Stealth Revolution*. Cambridge, MA: MIT Press.

Brown, W. (2019) *In the Ruins of Neoliberalism: The Rise of Antidemocratic Politics in the West*. New York, NY: Columbia University Press.

Brunson, R.K. and Miller, J. (2005) 'Young black men and urban policing in the United States', *British Journal of Criminology*, 46(4): 613–40.

Burke, M.E. (1994) 'Homosexuality as deviance: the case of the gay police officer', *British Journal of Criminology*, 34: 192–203.

Butler Committee (1975) 'Report of the Committee on Mentally Abnormal Offenders', Home Office, Department of Health and Social Security, Cmnd, 6244.

Butler, I. and Drakeford, M. (2001) 'Which Blair project? Communitarianism, social authoritarianism and social work', *Journal of Social Work*, 1(1): 7–19.

Cameron, D. (2010) 'Big Society Speech', www.gov.uk/government/speeches/big-society-speech

Cameron, D. (2015a) 'My vision for a smarter state', www.gov.uk/government/speeches/prime-minister-my-vision-for-a-smarter-state

Cameron, D. (2015b) 'David Cameron's conference speech in full', https://www.bbc.co.uk/news/av/uk-politics-34462710

Cammett, A. (2014) 'Deadbeat dads & welfare queens: how metaphor shapes poverty law', *Boston College Journal of Law & Social Justice*, 34: 233–65.

Campbell, S. (2002) *A Review of Anti-Social Behaviour Orders*, Home Office Research Study 236. London: Home Office.

Carrabine, E. (1998) 'Power, discourse and resistance: An analysis of the Strangeways prison riot', doctoral dissertation, University of Salford, UK.

Carrabine, E. (2005) 'Prison riots, social order and the problem of legitimacy', *British Journal of Criminology*, 45(6): 896–913.

Carvalho, H. (2017a) 'Liberty and insecurity in the criminal law: lessons from Thomas Hobbes', *Criminal Law and Philosophy*, 11(2): 249–71.

Carvalho, H. (2017b) *The Preventive Turn in Criminal Law*. Oxford: Oxford University Press.

Casefile: True Crime Podcast (2017) Case 37: The Yorkshire Ripper (Part 3), *Mixcloud*, www.mixcloud.com/casefiletruecrimepodcast/case-37-the-yorkshire-ripper-part-3/

Caspi, A., Houts, R.M., Belsky, D.W., Harrington, H., Hogan, S., Ramrakha, S., Poulton, R. and Moffitt, T.E. (2016) 'Childhood forecasting of a small segment of the population with large economic burden', *Nature Human Behaviour*, 1(1): 1–10.

Cathcart, B. (2012) *The Case of Stephen Lawrence*. London: Penguin.

Cavadino, M. and Dignan, J. (2006) *Penal Systems: A Comparative Approach*. London: Sage.

Centre for Welfare Reform (2015) *A Fair Society*. Sheffield: Centre for Welfare Reform, www.centreforwelfarereform.org

Chang, H.J. (2010) *Things They Don't Tell You About Capitalism*. London: Bloomsbury.

Christie, N. (1986) 'The ideal victim', in E.A. Fattah (ed) *From Crime Policy to Victim Policy*. London: Palgrave Macmillan, pp 17–30.

Clark, T. (2011) 'Why was Myra Hindley evil?', paper presented at the York Deviancy Conference, 'Critical Perspectives on Crime, Deviance, Disorder and Social Harm', July.

Clarke, J. (2008) 'Living with/in and without neo-liberalism', *Focaal*, 51: 135–47.

Clarke, J. and Newman, J. (1997) *The Managerial State*. London: Sage.

Cohen, N. (2002) 'How Blair put 30,000 more in jail', www.newstatesman.com/node/194579.

Cohen, S. (2002) *Folk Devils and Moral Panics*. London: Routledge.

Coid, J.W. (1992) 'DSM-III diagnosis in criminal psychopaths: a way forward', *Criminal Behaviour and Mental Health*, 2(2): 78–94.

Colvin, M. (1981) 'The Contradictions of Control: Prisons in Class Society', *Insurgent Sociologist*, 10/11: 33–46.

Colvin, M. (1992) *The Penitentiary in Crisis: From Accommodation to Riot in New Mexico*. Albany, NY: State University of New York Press.

Commission on Social Justice, The (1994) *Social Justice: Strategies for National Renewal*. London: Vintage.

Conservatives (2007) 'It's time to inspire Britain's teenagers: National Citizen Service for the 21st century: a six-week programme for every school leaver', http://conservativehome.blogs.com/interviews/files/timetoinspire.pdf

Crossley, S. (2015) *The Troubled Families Programme: The Perfect Social Policy?* London: Centre for Crime and Justice Studies.

Crossley, S. (2016) 'The Troubled Families Programme: in, for and against the state', *Social Policy Review*, 28: 127–46.

Crossley, S. (2017) *In Their Place: The Imagined Geographies of Poverty*. London: Pluto Press.

Cummins, I. (2016a) 'Reading Wacquant: social work and advanced marginality', *European Journal of Social Work*, 19(2): 263–74.

Cummins, I. (2016b) *Mental Health and the Criminal Justice System: A Social Work Perspective*. Northwich: Critical Publishing.

Cummins, I. (2018) *Poverty, Inequality and Social Work: The Impact of Neoliberalism and Austerity Politics on Welfare Provision*. Bristol: Policy Press.

Cummins, I., Foley, M. and King, M. (2019) *Serial Killers and the Media: The Moors Murders Legacy*. London: Springer.

Davis, M. (2006) *City of Quartz: Excavating the Future in Los Angeles* (new edn). London: Verso Books.

DCLG (Department for Communities and Local Government) (2012) 'The Troubled Families Programme. Financial framework for the Troubled Families Programme's payment-by-results scheme for local authorities', www.gov.uk/government/publications/the-troubled-families-programme-financial-framework

Deacon, A. (2000) 'Learning from the US? The influence of American ideas upon "New Labour" thinking on welfare reform', *Policy & Politics*, 28(1): 5–18.

Department for Communities and Local Government (2016) *National Evaluation of the Troubled Families Programme: Process evaluation final report*. London: Her Majesty's Stationery Office

Dorey, P. (2015) 'A farewell to alms: Thatcherism's legacy of inequality', *British Politics*, 10(1): 79–98.

Dorling, D., Rigby, J., Wheeler, B., Ballas, D., Thomas, B., Fahmy, E., Gordon, D. and Lupton, R. (2007) *Poverty, Wealth and Place in Britain, 1968 to 2005*. Bristol: Policy Press for the Joseph Rowntree Foundation.

Drucker, E. (2011) *A Plagues of Prisons: The Epidemiology of Mass Incarceration in America*. New York, NY: New Press.

Dunn, B. (2017) 'Against neoliberalism as a concept', *Capital & Class*, 41(3): 435–54.

Durkheim, E. (2006) *Durkheim: Essays on Morals and Education* (vol 1). Abingdon: Taylor & Francis.

Dwyer, P., Scullion, L., Jones, K., McNeill, J. and Stewart, A.B. (2019) 'Work, welfare, and wellbeing: the impacts of welfare conditionality on people with mental health impairments in the UK', *Social Policy & Administration*, 54(2): 1–16.

Emejulu, A. and Bassel, L. (2015) 'Minority women, austerity and activism', *Race & Class*, 57(2): 86–95.

Etzioni, A. (1993) *The Spirit of Community: The Reinvention of American Society*. New York, NY: Simon and Schuster.

Fallon, P., Bluglass, R., Edwards, B. and Daniels, G. (1999) *Report of the Committee of Inquiry into the Personality Disorder Unit, Ashworth Special Hospital* (vol 2). London: Stationery Office.

Farrall, S. and Hay, C. (2010) 'Not so tough on crime? Why weren't the Thatcher governments more radical in reforming the criminal justice system?', *The British Journal of Criminology*, 50(3): 550–69.

Farrall, S. and Jennings, W. (2012) 'Policy feedback and the criminal justice agenda: an analysis of the economy, crime rates, politics and public opinion in post-war Britain', *Contemporary British History*, 26(4): 467–88.

Finney, A. (2004) 'Perceptions of changing crime levels', in S. Nicholas and A. Walker (eds) *Crime in England and Wales 2002/2003 Supplementary Volume 2: Crime, Disorder and the Criminal Justice System – Public Attitudes and Perceptions*. London: Home Office Research and Statistics Directorate, pp 25–40.

Fischer, B.A. (2000) *The Reagan Reversal: Foreign Policy and the End of the Cold War*. Columbia, MO: University of Missouri Press.

Flint, J. (2019) 'Encounters with the centaur state: advanced urban marginality and the practices and ethics of welfare sanctions regimes', *Urban Studies*, 56(1): 249–65.

Foucault, M. (1982) 'The subject and power', *Critical Inquiry*, 8(4): 777–95.

Foucault, M. (2008) *The Birth of Biopolitics: Lectures at the College de France, 1978–79*. New York, NY: Palgrave.

Foucault, M. (2012) *Discipline and Punish: The Birth of the Prison*. London: Routledge Vintage.

Fraser, N. (2009) 'Capitalism, feminism, and the cunning of history', *New Left Review*, 56: 97–117.

Fraser, N. (2016) 'Progressive neoliberalism versus reactionary populism: a choice that feminists should refuse', *NORA – Nordic Journal of Feminist and Gender Research*, 24(4): 281–4.

Fraser, N. (2017a) 'From Progressive Neoliberalism to Trump—and Beyond', *American Affairs*, 1(4): 46–64.

Fraser, N. (2017b) 'Progressive neoliberalism versus reactionary populism: a Hobson's choice', in H. Geiselberger (ed) *The Great Regression*. Cambridge: Polity Press.

Friedman, M. (2009) *Capitalism and Freedom*. Chicago, IL: University of Chicago Press.

Fukuyama, F. (1992) *The End of History and the Last Man*. New York, NY: Simon and Schuster.

Fukuyama, F. (2018) *Identity: The Demand for Dignity and the Politics of Resentment.* New York, NY: Farrar, Straus and Giroux.

Gamble, A. (1994) *The Free Economy and the Strong State: The Politics of Thatcherism.* Basingstoke: Macmillan International Higher Education.

Garland, D. (1996) 'The Limits of the Sovereign State Strategies of Crime Control in Contemporary Society', *The British Journal of Criminology*, 36(4): 445–71.

Garland, D. (2001) *The Culture of Control: Crime and Social Order in Contemporary Society.* Oxford: Oxford University Press.

Garland, D. (2004) 'Beyond the culture of control', *Critical Review of International and Political Philosophy*, 7(2): 160–89.

Garland, D. (2014) 'The welfare state: a fundamental dimension of modern government', *European Journal of Sociology*, 55(3): 327–64.

Garland, D. (2018) 'Theoretical advances and problems in the sociology of punishment', *Punishment & Society*, 20(1): 8–33.

Garrett, P.M. (2007) 'Making social work more Bourdieusian: why the social professions should critically engage with the work of Pierre Bourdieu', *European Journal of Social Work*, 10(2): 225–43.

Garrett, P.M. (2015) 'Confronting neoliberal penality: placing prison reform and critical criminology at the core of social work's social justice agenda', *Journal of Social Work* 16(1): 83–103.

Garrett, P.M. (2017) 'Keywords: "welfare dependency" in the United Kingdom', *Journal of Progressive Human Services*, 28(2): 51–4.

Garrett, P.M. (2019) 'Revisiting "The birth of biopolitics": Foucault's account of neoliberalism and the remaking of social policy', *Journal of Social Policy*, 48(3): 469–87.

Garthwaite, K. (2016) *Hunger Pains: Life Inside Foodbank Britain.* Bristol: Policy Press.

Gentleman, A. (2019) *The Windrush Betrayal: Exposing the Hostile Environment.* London: Guardian Faber Publishing.

Giddens, A. (1998) *The Third Way: The Renewal of Social Democracy.* Cambridge: Polity Press.

Gilliam, F.D., Jr (1999) 'The "welfare queen" experiment: how viewers react to images of African-mothers on welfare', *The Nieman Foundation for Journalism*, 53: 112–19.

Gilmour, I. (1992) *Dancing with Dogma: Britain under Thatcherism.* London: Simon & Schuster.

Gilroy, P. (1982) 'The myth of black criminality', in R. Miliband (ed) *The Socialist Register.* London: Merlin.

Gilroy, P. (2013) *There Ain't No Black in the Union Jack.* Abingdon: Routledge.

Giroux, H. (2011) 'Neoliberalism and the death of the social state: remembering Walter Benjamin's Angel of History', *Social Identities: Journal for the Study of Race, Nation and Culture*, 17(4): 587–601.

Giroux, H. (2017) 'Trump's Neo-Nazis and the Rise of Illiberal Democracy', *TruthOut*, 16 August, https://truthout.org/articles/neo-nazis-in-charlottesville-and-the-rise-of-illiberal-democracy/

Goffman, E. (2009) *Stigma: Notes on the Management of Spoiled Identity*. New York, NY: Simon and Schuster.

Gottschalk, M. (2006) *The Prison and the Gallows: The politics of mass incarceration in America*. Cambridge: Cambridge University Press.

Gough, I. (1979) *The Political Economy of the Welfare State*. Basingstoke: Macmillan International Higher Education.

Gough, I. (1980) 'Thatcherism and the welfare state: Britain is experiencing the most far-reaching experiment in "new right" politics in the Western world', *Marxism Today*, July 1980: 7–12.

Gramsci, A. (1971) *Selections from the Prison Notebooks* (eds and trans Q. Hoare and G. Nowell Smith). New York, NY: International Publishers.

Gray, J. (2013) *Hayek on Liberty*. Abingdon: Routledge.

Grover, C. and Soothill, K. (1999) 'British serial killing: towards a structural explanation', in M. Brogden (ed) *The British Criminology Conferences: Selected Proceedings* (vol 2), July, http://britsoccrim.org/volume2/008.pdf.

Guardian (1999) 'Straw unveils plan to lock up "dangerous" mental patients before they commit crimes', 19 July, www.theguardian.com/uk/1999/jul/19/2

Guardian (2017) 'Sex offender treatment scheme led to increase in reoffending', 30 June, www.theguardian.com/uk-news/2017/jun/30/sex-offenders-on-group-treatment-programme-more-likely-to-reoffend

Haggerty, K.D. (2009) 'Modern serial killers', *Crime, Media, Culture*, 5(2): 168–87.

Hague, W. (2007) *William Wilberforce: The Life of the Great Anti-Slave Trade Campaigner*. Houghton: Mifflin Harcourt.

Halcrow, M. (1989) *Keith Joseph: A Single Mind*. Basingstoke: Macmillan.

Hall, C. (2016) 'Writing history, making "race": slave-owners and their stories', *Australian Historical Studies*, 47(3): 365–80.

Hall, S. (1979) 'The great moving right show', *Marxism Today*, 23(1): 14–20.

Hall, S. (1997) *Representation: Cultural representations and signifying practices*, volume 2, London: Sage.

Hall, S. (1998) 'The great moving nowhere show', *Marxism Today*, 1(1): 9–14.

Hall, S. (2011) 'The neo-liberal revolution', *Cultural Studies*, 25(6): 705–28.

Hall, S. and Wilson, D. (2014) 'New foundations: pseudo-pacification and special liberty as potential cornerstones for a multi-level theory of homicide and serial murder', *European Journal of Criminology*, 11(5): 635–55.

Hall, S., Critcher, C., Jefferson, T., Clarke, J. and Roberts, B. (2013) *Policing the Crisis* (35th anniversary edn). Basingstoke: Palgrave.

Halliday, J. (2001a) *The Halliday Report: Making Punishments Work: A Review of the Sentencing Framework for England & Wales*. London: HMSO.

Halliday, J. (2001b) *Making Punishment Work: Report of a Review of the Sentencing Framework for England and Wales*. London: Home Office Communication Directorate.

Haney-López, I. (2014) *Dog Whistle Politics: How Coded Racial Appeals Have Reinvented Racism and Wrecked the Middle Class*. Oxford: Oxford University Press.

Harvey, D. (2005) *A Brief History of Neoliberalism*. Oxford: Oxford University Press.

Harvey, D. (2012) *Rebel Cities: From the Right to the City to the Urban Revolution*. London: Verso.

Hay, C. (1995) 'Mobilization through interpellation: James Bulger, juvenile crime and the construction of a moral panic', *Social & Legal Studies*, 4(2): 197–223.

Hay, C. and Farrall, S. (2014) 'Interrogating and conceptualising the legacy of Thatcherism', in S. Farrall and C. Hay (eds) *The Legacy of Thatcherism: Assessing and Exploring Thatcherite Social and Economic Policies*. Oxford: Oxford University Press, pp 3–31.

Hayek, F.A. (2014) *The Road to Serfdom: Text and Documents: The Definitive Edition*. London: Routledge.

Hayek, F.A. (2018) *New Studies in Philosophy, Politics, Economics, and the History of Ideas*. Chicago, IL: University of Chicago Press.

Hills, J. (2015) *The Coalition's Record on Cash Transfers, Poverty and Inequality 2010–2015*. London: London School of Economics and Political Science, Centre for Analysis of Social Exclusion.

Hills, J. (2017) *Good Times, Bad Times (Revised Edition): The Welfare Myth of Them and Us*. Bristol: Policy Press.

Hinton, E. (2016) *From the War on Poverty to the War on Crime*. Cambridge, MA: Harvard University Press.

Hinton, E. (2018) *An Unjust Burden: The Disparate Treatment of Black Americans in the Criminal Justice System*. New York, NY: Vera Institute of Justice.

Hirsch, S. (2018) *In the Shadow of Enoch Powell: Race, Locality and Resistance*. Manchester: Manchester University Press.

Hirschman, A. (1991) *The Rhetoric of Reaction: Perversity, Futility, Jeopardy*. Cambridge, MA: Harvard University Press.

Her Majesty's Chief Inspector of Prisons (2019) 'HM Chief Inspector of Prisons' annual report for 2018–19', https://assets.publishing.service. gov.uk/government/uploads/system/uploads/attachment_data/file/ 814689/hmip-annual-report-2018-19.pdf

Her Majesty's Inspectorate of Constabulary (HMIC) (1999) *Police Integrity: Securing and Maintaining Public Confidence*. London: Home Office.

Hobbes, T. (2016) *Thomas Hobbes: Leviathan (Longman Library of Primary Sources in Philosophy)*. London: Routledge.

Hobsbawm, E. (1994) *The Age of Extremes: A History of the World, 1914–1991*, New York, NY: Vintage.

Holdaway, S. (1983) *Inside the British Police*. Oxford: Blackwells.

Holdaway, S. (1986) 'Police and social work relations – problems and possibilities', *British Journal of Social Work*, 16(2): 137–60.

Home Office (1990) *Crime, Justice and Protecting the Public*. London: HMSO.

Home Office (2003) *Together: Tackling Anti-Social Behaviour*. London: Home Office.

Home Office and Department of Health (1999) *Managing Dangerous People with Severe Personality Disorder: Proposals for Policy Development*. London: HMSO.

House of Commons Justice Committee (2012) *Joint Enterprise: Eleventh Report of Session 2010–12*, https://publications.parliament.uk/pa/ cm201012/cmselect/cmjust/1597/1597.pdf.

Ipsos MORI (2015) 'National Citizen Service 2014 evaluation', www. ipsos-mori.com/researchpublications/publications/1784/National-Citizen-Service-2014-Evaluation.aspx

Jarecki, E. (2012) 'The house I live in' (produced by M. Shopsin), Charlotte Street Films, New York.

Jeffery, B. (2011) *Anti-Matter: Michel Houellebecq and Depressive Realism*. London: Zero.

Jensen, T. (2014) 'Welfare commonsense, poverty porn and doxosophy', *Sociological Research Online*, 19(3): 1–7.

Jensen, T. and Tyler, I. (2015) ' "Benefits broods": the cultural and political crafting of anti-welfare common sense', *Critical Social Policy*, 35(4): 1–22.

Jones, D.W. (2017) 'Moral insanity and psychological disorder: the hybrid roots of psychiatry', *History of Psychiatry*, 28(3): 263–79.

Jones, T. and Newburn, T. (2007) *Policy Transfer and Criminal Justice: Exploring US Influence Over British Crime Control Policy*. Maidenhead: Open University Press.

Joseph Rowntree Foundation (2016) 'Monitoring poverty and social exclusion', www.npi.org.uk/files/7614/8111/0522/MPSE_Findings_2016.pdf

Karban, K. (2016) 'Developing a health inequalities approach for mental health social work', *British Journal of Social Work*, 47(3): 885–992.

Kerner Commission (1968) *The Kerner Report: The 1968 Report of the National Advisory Commission on Civil Disorders*. New York, NY: Pantheon.

Kirkup, J. and Winnett, R. (2012) 'Theresa May interview: "We're going to give illegal migrants a really hostile reception"', *The Telegraph*, 25 May, www.telegraph.co.uk/news/0/theresa-may-interview-going-give-illegal-migrants-really-hostile/

Kley, R. (1994) *Hayek's Social and Political Thought*. Oxford: Clarendon Press.

Kohler-Hausmann, J. (2015) 'Welfare crises, penal solutions, and the origins of the "welfare queen"', *Journal of Urban History*, 41(5): 756–71.

Krebs, B. (2010) 'Joint criminal enterprise', *The Modern Law Review*, 73(4): 578–604.

Krugman, P. (2015) 'The case for cuts was a lie. Why does Britain still believe it?', *Guardian*, 29 April, www.theguardian.com/business/ng-interactive/2015/apr/29/the-austerity-delusion

Kwarteng, K., Patel, P., Raab, D., Skidmore, C. and Truss, E. (2012) *Britannia Unchained*. London: Palgrave Macmillan.

Kynaston, D. (2008) *Austerity Britain, 1945–1951* (vol 1). London: Bloomsbury.

Kynaston, D. (2010) *Family Britain, 1951–1957*. London: Bloomsbury.

Kynaston, D. (2014) *Modernity Britain: 1957–1962*. London: Bloomsbury.

Labour Party (1997) *New Labour: Because Britain Deserves Better. Labour Party Manifesto, General Election 1997*. London: Labour Party.

Lacey, N. (2008) *The Prisoners' Dilemma: Political Economy and Punishment in Contemporary Democracies*. Cambridge: Cambridge University Press.

Lakoff, G. and Johnson, M. (1980) 'The metaphorical structure of the human conceptual system', *Cognitive Science*, 4(2): 195–208.

Lammy, D. (2017) *An Independent Review into the Treatment of, and Outcomes for, Black, Asian and Minority Ethnic Individuals in the Criminal Justice System.* London: National Audit Office.

Lancet, The (1999) 'The horrors of Ashworth', www.thelancet.com/journals/lancet/article/PIIS0140-6736(99)00015-X/fulltext

Larner, W. (2003) 'Neoliberalism?', *Environment and Planning D: Society and Space*, 21: 509–12.

Lawson, M. (1994) 'The making of blue Peter', *Independent*, 3 April, www.independent.co.uk/arts-entertainment/the-making-of-blue-peter-in-the-last-two-years-peter-lilley-has-shot-from-obscurity-to-euro-baiting-1367591.html

Lea, J. (1987) 'Left realism: a defence', *Contemporary Crises*, 11: 21–32.

Lea, J. (1992) 'The analysis of crime', in J. Young and R. Matthews (eds) *Rethinking Criminology: The Realist Debate.* London: Sage.

Lea, J. (2002) *Crime and Modernity.* London: Sage.

Lea, J. (2010) 'Left realism, community and state-building', *Crime, Law & Social Change*, 54(2): 141–58.

Lea, J. (2016) 'Left realism: a radical criminology for the current crisis', *International Journal for Crime, Justice and Social Democracy*, 5(3): 53.

Lea, J. and Young, J. (1993) *What is to Be Done about Law and Order?* London: Pluto Press.

Letelier, O. (1976) 'Economic "freedom's" awful toll: the "Chicago Boys" in Chile', *Review of Radical Political Economics*, 8(3): 44–52.

Leuchtenburg, W.E. (2009 [1963]) *Franklin D. Roosevelt and the New Deal: 1932–1940.* New York, NY: Harper Collins.

Levitas, R. (1996) 'The concept of social exclusion and the new Durkheimian hegemony', *Critical Social Policy*, 16(1): 5–20.

Levitas, R. (1998) *The Inclusive Society?* Basingstoke: Macmillan.

Levitas, R. (2012) 'There may be "trouble" ahead: what we know about those 120,000 "troubled" families', *Policy Response Series*, 3: 1–13.

Lewis, P., Newburn, T., Taylor, M., Mcgillivray, C., Greenhill, A., Frayman, H. and Proctor, R. (2011) 'Reading the riots: investigating England's summer of disorder', https://eprints.lse.ac.uk/46297/1/Reading%20the%20riots(published).pdf

Leyva, R. (2018) 'Towards a cognitive-sociological theory of subjectivity and habitus formation in neoliberal environments', *European Journal of Social Theory*, 22(2): 250–71.

Lianos, M. and Douglas, M. (2000) 'Dangerization and the end of deviance: the institutional environment', *British Journal of Criminology*, 40(2): 261–78.

Liebling, A. (2000) 'Prison officers, policing and the use of discretion', *Theoretical Criminology*, 4(3): 333–57.

Liebling, A. (2002) *Suicides in Prison*. Abingdon: Routledge.

Lipsky, M. (1980) *Street-Level Bureaucracy: Dilemmas of the Individual in Public Service*. New York, NY: Russell Sage Foundation.

Lister, R. (1998) 'From equality to social inclusion: New Labour and the welfare state', *Critical Social Policy*, 18(55): 215–25.

Lloyd, A. and Whitehead, P. (2018) 'Kicked to the curb: the triangular trade of neoliberal polity, social insecurity, and penal expulsion', *International Journal of Law, Crime and Justice*, 55: 60–9.

Loftus, B. (2009) *Police Culture in a Changing World*. Oxford: Oxford University Press.

Loftus, B. (2010) 'Police occupational culture: classic themes altered times', *Policing and Society*, 20(1): 1–20.

Lopez, G. (2018) 'California is using prison labor to fight its record wildfires', *Vox*, 9 August, www.vox.com/2018/8/9/17670494/california-prison-labor-mendocino-carr-ferguson-wildfires

López, T.M (2014) *The Winter of Discontent: Myth, Memory, and History* Oxford: Oxford University Press.

Macey, D. (1993) *The Lives of Michel Foucault*. New York, NY: Vintage.

Macintyre, D. (1993) 'Major on crime: "Condemn more, understand less"', *Independent*, 21 February, https://www.independent.co.uk/news/major-on-crime-condemn-more-understand-less-1474470.html

Macpherson, S.W. (1999) *The Stephen Lawrence Inquiry: Report of an Inquiry by Sir William Macpherson of Cluny*. London: HMSO.

Malcolm X (1965) *The Autobiography of Malcolm X (with the Assistance of Alex Haley)*. London: Penguin.

Malthus, T.R. (1985 [1798]) *An Essay on the Principle of Population*. London: Penguin Books.

Marmot, M. (2010) *Fair Society, Healthy Lives: The Marmot Review*. London: Department of Health, www.parliament.uk/documents/fair-society-healthy-lives-full-report.pdf

Marshall, K. (2008) *Not Seen. Not Heard. Not Guilty. The Rights and Status of the Children of Prisoners in Scotland*. Edinburgh: Scotland's Commissioner for Children and Young People.

Martinson, R. (1974) 'What works? Questions and answers about prison reform', *The Public Interest*, 35: 22–54.

Matthews, R. (2010) 'The construction of "So what?" criminology: A realist analysis', *Crime, Law and Social Change*, 54(2): 125–40.

Matthews, R. (2014) *Realist Criminology*. Basingstoke: Palgrave Macmillan.

McConnell, M. and Raikes, B. (2019) ' "It's not a case of he'll be home one day." The impact on families of sentences of imprisonment for public protection (IPP)', *Child Care in Practice*, 25(4): 349–66.

McKenzie, L. (2015) *Getting By: Estates, Class and Culture in Austerity Britain*. Bristol: Policy Press.

McLaughlin, E. (2007) *The New Policing*. London: Sage.

Mead, L. (1991) 'The new politics of the new poverty', *Public Interest*, 103: 3–20.

Mead, L. (1992) *The New Politics of Poverty: The Nonworking Poor in America*. New York, NY: Basic Books.

Miliband, D. (ed) (1994) *Reinventing the Left*. Cambridge: Polity Press.

Ministry of Justice (2014) 'Offender Management Statistics Quarterly Bulletin: July to September 2013, England and Wales', https://assets. publishing.service.gov.uk/government/uploads/system/uploads/ attachment_data/file/276074/omsq-q3-2013.pdf

Mirowski, P. (2013) *Never Let a Crisis Go to Waste: How Neoliberalism Survived the Financial Meltdown*. London: Verso.

Mirowski, P. (2014) 'The political movement that dared not speak its own name: The neoliberal thought collective under erasure', Institute for New Economic Thinking Working Paper Series, 23.

Mohan, J. (2012) 'Geographical foundations of the Big Society', *Environment and Planning A*, 44(5): 1121–7.

Moore, C. (2013) *Margaret Thatcher: The Authorized Biography, Volume One: Not for turning*. London: Penguin.

Morgan, N. (2014) *The Heroin Epidemic of the 1980s and 1990s and Its Effect on Crime Trends – Then and Now. Research Report 79*. London: Home Office.

Morrison, B. (1997) *As If: A Crime, a Trial, a Question of Childhood*. New York: Picador USA.

Muhammed, K.G. (2010) *The Condemnation of Blackness: Race, Crime, and the Making of Modern Urban America*. Cambridge, MA: Harvard University Press.

Mullen, P.E. (1999) 'Dangerous people with severe personality disorder: British proposals for managing them are glaringly wrong – and unethical', *British Medical Journal* 319, 1146–7.

Murray, C. (1990) *The Emerging British Underclass (Choice in Welfare)*. London: IEA.

Murray, C. (1994) *Losing Ground: American Social Policy, 1950–1980*. New York, NY: Basic Books.

Murray, C. (2012) *Coming Apart: The State of White America, 1960–2010*. New York, NY: Random House.

Mycock, A. and Tonge, J. (2011) 'A big idea for the Big Society? The advent of national citizen service', *The Political Quarterly*, 82(1): 56–66.

NACRO (2002) *Tackling Anti-Social Behaviour. Briefing.* London: NACRO.

NACRO (2006) *Youth Crime Briefing: Anti Social Behaviour Orders for 10–17 Year Olds and Overview.* London: NACRO.

Nelson, F. (2014) 'In defence of Channel 4's Benefits Street', https://blogs.spectator.co.uk/2014/01/in-defence-of-channel-4s-benefits-street/

Newburn, T. (2003) *Crime and Criminal Justice Policy.* London: Pearson Education.

Newburn, T. (2007) 'Tough on crime: penal policy in England and Wales', *Crime and Justice*, 36: 425–70.

Newburn, T. (2014) 'The 2011 England riots in recent historical perspective', *British Journal of Criminology*, 55(1): 39–64.

Norman, J. (2010) *The Big Society; The Anatomy of the New Politics.* London: Legend Press Ltd.

North, P. (2011) 'Geographies and utopias of Cameron's Big Society', *Social & Cultural Geography*, 12(8): 817–27.

Nozick, R. (1974) *Anarchy, State and Utopia.* Oxford: Blackwell.

O'Connor, A. (2001) *Poverty Knowledge: Social Science, Social Policy, and the Poor in Twentieth Century U.S. History.* Princeton, NJ: Princeton University Press.

O'Neill, M. and McCarthy, D. (2014) '(Re)Negotiating police culture through partnership working: trust, compromise and the "new" pragmatism', *Criminology and Criminal Justice*, 1(2): 143–59.

O'Neill, M., Marks, M. and Singh, A.-M. (eds) (2007) *Police Occupational Culture: New Debates and Directions.* Amsterdam: Elsevier JAI Press.

Owusu-Bempah, A. (2017) 'Race and policing in historical context: dehumanization and the policing of black people in the 21st century', *Theoretical Criminology*, 21(1): 23–34.

Oxfam (2103) 'Truth and lies about poverty: ending comfortable myths about poverty', www.oxfam.org

Parsons, A.E. (2018) *From Asylum to Prison: Deinstitutionalization and the Rise of Mass Incarceration after 1945.* Chapel Hill, NC: UNC Press Books.

Pashukanis, E.B. (1978) *Law and Marxism: A General Theory* (trans B. Einhorn). London: Ink Links.

Peck, J. and Theodore, N. (2010) 'Mobilizing policy: models, methods and mutations', *Geoforum*, 41(2): 169–74.

Penfold-Mounce, R., Beer, D. and Burrows, R. (2011) '*The wire* as social science-fiction?', *Sociology*, 45(1): 152–67.

Perkins, A. (2016) *The Welfare Trait: How State Benefits Affect Personality.* London: Springer.

Pettigrew, M. (2016) 'Myra Hindley: murderer, prisoner, policy architect. The development of whole life prison terms in England & Wales', *International Journal of Law, Crime and Justice*, 47: 97–105.

Pfaff, J. (2017) *Locked In: The True Causes of Mass Incarceration – and How to Achieve Real Reform.* New York, NY: Basic Books.

Pidd, H. and Perraudin, F. (2017) 'Gang members guilty of "hunting down" and killing 18-year-old in street', *Guardian*, 8 August, www.theguardian.com/uk-news/2017/aug/08/gang-members-guilty-of-hunting-down-and-killing-18-year-old-in-street

Pilkington, E. (1988) *Beyond the Mother Country: West Indians and the Notting Hill white riots.* London: IB Tauris & Company Limited.

Piven, F.F. and Cloward, R. (2012) *Regulating the Poor: The Functions of Public Welfare.* New York: Vintage.

Polanyi, K. (1957) *The Great Transformation.* Boston: Beacon Publishing.

Pollitt, C. and Bouckaert, G. (2004) *Public Management Reform: A Comparative Analysis.* Oxford: Oxford University Press.

Powell, M. (ed) (1999) *New Labour, New Welfare State? The 'Third Way' in British Social Policy.* Bristol: Policy Press.

Prison Reform Trust (2016) 'Rising self-harm rates show growing despair amongst IPP prisoners still stuck behind bars', www.prisonreformtrust.org.uk/PressPolicy/News/vw/1/ItemID/335

Prison Reform Trust (2018) 'UK tops European league table of numbers in indefinite detention', www.prisonreformtrust.org.uk/PressPolicy/News/vw/1/ItemID/601

Prison Reform Trust (2019) *Prison: the facts*, www.prisonreformtrust.org.uk/Portals/0/Documents/Bromley%20Briefings/Prison%20the%20facts%20Summer%202019.pdf

Ramsden, E. and Adams, J. (2009) 'Escaping the laboratory: the rodent experiments of John B. Calhoun & their cultural influence', *Journal of Social History*, 42(3): 761–92.

Rawlinson, K. and Gentleman, A. (2019) 'Home Office Windrush report damns hostile environment policy', *Guardian*, 27 June, www.theguardian.com/uk-news/2019/jun/27/home-office-windrush-report-damns-hostile-environment-policy

Reed, J. (1992) *Review of Health and Social Services for Mentally Disordered Offenders and Others Requiring Similar Services* (vol 1). London: HMSO.

Riddell, P. (1991) *The Thatcher Era and Its Legacy.* Oxford: Blackwell.

Rogers, C. (2014) 'From union legislation to financial reform: a reflection on Thatcherism, capital and the British state', *Capital & Class*, 38(2): 289–302.

Rose, N. (1994) 'Medicine, historry and the present', in C. Jones and R. Porter (eds) *Reassessing Foucault: Power, Medicine and the Body*. London: Routledge.

Royal College of Physicians (1908) *Report of the Royal Commission on the care and control of the feeble-minded* (vol 3). London: HMSO.

Ryan, F. (2019) *Crippled: Austerity and the Demonization of Disabled People*. London: Verso.

Sainsbury Centre for Mental Health (2008) *In the Dark: The Mental Health Implications of Imprisonment for Public Protection*. London: Sainsbury Centre for Mental Health.

Sandberg, S. (2013) *Lean In: Women, Work, and the Will to Lead*. New York, NY: Alfred A. Knopf.

Sandbrook, D. (2011) *State of Emergency: The Way We Were: Britain, 1970–1974*. London: Penguin.

Saul, J.M. (2017) 'Racial figleaves, the shifting boundaries of the permissible, and the rise of Donald Trump', *Philosophical Topics*, 45(2): 97–116.

Savage, M. (2015) *Social Class in the 21st Century*. London: Penguin.

Scarman, J., Lord (1981) *The Brixton Disorders, 10–12th April (1981)*. London: HMSO.

Schone, J.M. (2000) 'The hardest case of all: Myra Hindley, life sentences, and the rule of law', *International Journal of the Sociology of Law (Print)*, 28(4): 273–89.

Schrag, P. (2004) *Paradise Lost: California's Experience, America's Future: Updated with a New Preface*. Berkeley, CA: University of California Press.

Scott, D. (2007) 'New legitimacy? The "making punishment work" agenda and the limits of penal reform', in R. Roberts and W. McMahon (eds) *Social Justice and Criminal Justice*. London: Harm & Society Foundation, pp 71–81, http://oro.open.ac.uk/51603/

Scraton, P., Sim, J. and Skidmore, P. (1991) *Prisons Under Protest*. Buckingham: Open University Press.

Seddon, T. (2007) *Punishment and Madness: Governing Prisoners with Mental Health Problems*. Basingstoke: Routledge-Cavendish.

Sered, D. (2019) *Until We Reckon: Violence, Mass Incarceration, and a Road to Repair*. New York, NY: The New Press.

Sereny, G. (1995) *The Case of Mary Bell: A Portrait of a Child Who Murdered*. London: Pimilico.

Shildrick, T. and MacDonald, R. (2012) *Poverty and Insecurity: Life in Low-Pay, No-Pay Britain*. Bristol: Policy Press.

Shildrick, T., Blackman, S. and MacDonald, R. (2009) 'Young people, class and place', *Journal of Youth Studies*, 12(5): 457–65.

Shore, C. and Wright, S. (2015) 'Governing by numbers: audit culture, rankings and the new world order', *Social Anthropology*, 23(1): 22–8.

Simon, J. (2001) 'Governing through crime metaphors', *Brook Law Review*, 67(4): 1035–69.

Simon, J. (2007) *Governing Through Crime: How the War on Crime Transformed American Democracy and Created a Culture of Fear.* Oxford: Oxford University Press.

Simon, J. (2010a) 'Do these prisons make me look fat? Moderating the USA's consumption of punishment', *Theoretical Criminology*, 14(3): 257–72.

Simon, J. (2010b) 'How should we punish murder', *Marquette Law Review*, 94: 1243 –313.

Simon, J. (2014) *Mass Incarceration on Trial: A Remarkable Court Decision and the Future of Prisons in America.* New York, NY: The New Press.

Simon, J. and Feeley, M. (2003) 'The form and limits of the new penology', in T. Blomberg and S. Cohen (eds) *Punishment and Social Control*, 2nd edition. New York, NY: Aldine de Gruyter.

Skelcher, C. (2000) 'Changing images of the state: overloaded, hollowed-out, congested', *Public Policy and Administration*, 15(3): 3–19.

Skogan, W. (2008) 'Why reforms fail', *Policing and Society*, 18(1): 23–34.

Slater, T. (2014) 'The myth of "Broken Britain": welfare reform and the production of ignorance', *Antipode*, 46(4): 948–69.

Slater, T. (2018) 'The invention of the "sink estate": consequential categorisation and the UK housing crisis', *The Sociological Review*, 66(4): 877–97.

Smith, A. (2010) *The Theory of Moral Sentiments.* London: Penguin.

Smith, D. (2005) 'Probation and Social Work', *The British Journal of Social Work* 35(5): 621–37.

Somers, M. (2008) *Genealogies of Citizenship: Markets, Statelessness, and the Rights to Have Rights.* Cambridge: Cambridge University Press. *Sunday Times* (1993) 'Editorial', 28 November.

Somers, M.R. and Block, F. (2005) 'From poverty to perversity: ideas, markets, and institutions over 200 years of welfare debate', *American Sociological Review*, 70(2): 260–87.

Squires, P. (2006) 'New Labour and the politics of antisocial behaviour', *Critical Social Policy*, 26(1): 144–68.

Standing, G. (2011) *The Precariat: The New Dangerous Class.* London: Bloomsbury Academic.

Stedman-Jones, D. (2012) *Masters of the Universe: Hayek, Friedman and the Birth of Neoliberal Politics.* Princeton, NJ: Princeton University Press. *Sunday Times* (1993) 'Editorial', 28 November.

Tam, H. (2011) 'The big con: reframing the state/society debate', *Public Policy Research*, 18(1): 30–40.

Taylor, C. (2004) *Modern Social Imaginaries*. Durham, NC: Duke University Press.

Taylor-Gooby, P. (2012) 'Overview: resisting welfare state restructuring in the UK', *Journal of Poverty and Social Justice*, 20: 119–32.

Thompson, H.A. (2017) *Blood in the Water: The Attica Prison Uprising of 1971 and Its Legacy*. New York, NY: Pantheon Books

Thorpe, K. and Wood, M. (2004) 'Attitudes to anti-social behaviour', in S. Nicholas and A. Walker (eds) *Crime in England and Wales 2002/ 2003 Supplementary Volume 2: Crime, Disorder and the Criminal Justice System – Public Attitudes and Perceptions*. London: Home Office Research and Statistics Directorate, pp 65–73.

Timmins, N. (2001) *The Five Giants: A Biography of the Welfare State*. London: Harper Collins.

Todd, S. (2014) *The People: The Rise and Fall of the Working Class, 1910–2010*. London: Hachette.

Tyler, I. (2008) '"Chav mum chav scum": class disgust in contemporary Britain', *Feminist Media Studies*, 8(1): 17–34.

Tyler, I. (2018a) 'Resituating Erving Goffman: from stigma power to black power', *The Sociological Review*, 66(4): 744–65.

Tyler, I. (2018b) 'Deportation nation: Theresa May's hostile environment', *Journal for the Study of British Cultures*, 25(1), https:// eprints.lancs.ac.uk/id/eprint/125439/

United Nations Committee on the Rights of Persons with Disabilities (CRPD) (2017) *Concluding Observations on the Initial Report of the United Kingdom of Great Britain and Northern Ireland*. Geneva: United Nations Office of the High Commissioner for Human Rights.

Useem, B. and Kimball, P. (1991) *States of Siege: US Prison Riots, 1971–1986*. Oxford: Oxford University Press.

Venugopal, R. (2015) 'Neoliberalism as concept', *Economy and Society*, 44(2): 165–87.

Vera (nd) 'Ending Mass Incarceration', www.vera.org/ ending-mass-incarceration.

Wacquant, L. (2002) 'From slavery to mass incarceration', *New Left Review*, 13(1): 41–60.

Wacquant, L. (2007) 'Territorial stigmatization in the age of advanced marginality', *Thesis Eleven*, 91: 66–77.

Wacquant, L. (2008) *Urban Outcasts: A Comparative Sociology of Advanced Marginality*. Cambridge. Polity Press.

Wacquant, L. (2009a) *Prisons of Poverty*. Minneapolis, MN: UM Press.

Wacquant, L. (2009b) *Punishing the Poor: The Neoliberal Government of Social Insecurity*. Durham, NC: Duke University Press.

Wacquant, L. (2010) 'Crafting the neoliberal state: workfare, prisonfare, and social insecurity', *Sociological Forum*, 25(2): 197–220.

Wacquant, L. (2012) 'Three steps to a historical anthropology of actually existing neoliberalism', *Social Anthropology*, 20(1): 66–79.

Wacquant, L. (2013) 'The wedding of workfare and prisonfare in the 21st century: responses to critics and commentators', in P. Squires and J. Lea (eds) *Criminalisation and Advanced Marginality: Critically Exploring the Work of Loïc Wacquant*. Bristol: Policy Press, pp 243–58.

Wacquant, L. (2016) 'Revisiting territories of relegation: class, ethnicity and state in the making of advanced marginality', *Urban Studies*, 53(6): 1077–88.

Waddington, D. (1992) *Contemporary Issues in Public Disorder*. London: Routledge.

Wattis, L. (2017) 'Revisiting the Yorkshire Ripper murders: interrogating gender violence, sex work, and justice', *Feminist Criminology*, 12(1): 3–21.

Wattis, L. (2019) 'Violence, emotion and place: the case of five murders involving sex workers', *Crime, Media, Culture*, 16(2): 201–19.

Webb, S. (2006) *Social Work in a Risk Society: Social and Political Perspectives*. Basingstoke: Palgrave Macmillan.

Welshman, J. (2013) *Underclass: A History of the Excluded since 1880*. London: Bloomsbury.

Wilding, P. (1992) 'The British welfare state: Thatcherism's enduring legacy', *Policy & Politics*, 20(3): 201–12.

Wilkinson, R. and Pickett, K. (2009) *The Spirit Level: Why Equality is Better for Everyone*. London: Penguin.

Williams, E. (2014) *Capitalism and Slavery*. Chapel Hill, NC: UNC Press Books.

Williams, P. and Clarke, B. (2016) *Dangerous Associations: Joint Enterprise, Gangs and Racism*. London: Centre for Crime and Justice Studies.

Wills, C. (2017) *Lovers and Strangers: An Immigrant History of Post-War Britain*. London: Penguin.

Wilson, J.Q. and Kelling, G.L. (1982) 'Broken windows', *Atlantic Monthly*, 249(3): 29–38.

Wilson, W.J. (2011) *When Work Disappears: The World of the New Urban Poor*. London: Vintage.

Wilson, W.J. (2012) *The Truly Disadvantaged: The Inner City, the Underclass, and Public Policy*. Chicago, IL: University of Chicago Press.

Windlesham, D. (1993) *Responses to Crime Volume 2: Penal Policy in the Making*. Oxford: Clarendon.

Wintour, P. (2013) 'Cameron refuses to endorse Gove's criticism of food bank users', *Guardian*, 11 September, www.theguardian.com/society/2013/sep/11/david-cameron-michael-gove-food-banks

Woolf, L.J. (1991) *Prison Disturbances April 1990: Report of an Inquiry.* London: HMSO.

Wright, E.O. (1997) *Class Counts.* Cambridge: Cambridge University Press.

Wright Mills, C. (2000) *The Sociological Imagination.* Oxford: Oxford University Press.

York, S. (2018) 'The "hostile environment": how Home Office immigration policies and practices create and perpetuate illegality', *Journal of Immigration, Asylum and Nationality Law,* 32(4): 363–84.

Young, H. (2013) *One of Us.* London: Pan Macmillan.

Young, J. (1991) 'Left realism and the priorities of crime control', in K. Stenson and D. Cowell (eds) *The Politics of Crime Control.* London: Sage, pp 146–60.

Young, J. (1992) 'Ten points of realism', in J. Young and R. Matthews (eds) *Rethinking Criminology: The Realist Debate.* London: Sage, pp 24–68.

Young, J. (1999) *The Exclusive Society: Social Exclusion, Crime and Difference in Late Modernity.* London: Sage.

Zimring, F.E., Hawkins, G. and Kamin, S. (2001) *Punishment and Democracy: Three Strikes and You're Out in California.* Oxford: Oxford University Press.

Zizek, S. (2011) 'Shoplifters of the world unite!', *London Review of Books,* www.lrb.co.uk/2011/08/19/slavoj-zizek/shoplifters-of-the-world-unite

Index

www.ingramcontent.com/pod-product-compliance
Lightning Source LLC
Chambersburg PA
CBHW070932030426
42336CB00014BA/2641